Seven Secrets
to a
Successful Divorce

what every woman needs to know

Christina Rowe

JGA Publishers

This book is not legal advice—it is just practical advice and observations. The laws vary by State. For legal advice, you should always consult a lawyer licensed to practice law in your State.

JGA Publishers
3171 Route 9 North, #321
Old Bridge, NJ 08857

For more information:
www.secretsofdivorce.com

Cover design by Dunn+Associates Design
Photograph by Michael Benabib, Digital Headshots NYC
Hair done by Veronica Sunyak, Vogue Hair & Nails

ISBN: 0-9787562-0-7

10987654321

Printed in the United States of America

Other Product Offerings from Christina Rowe

Christina has a variety of audio courses, ebooks, DVD packages, and newsletters available. Check out: www.secretsofdivorce.com

If you're interested in private coaching with Christina, send an email to: christina@secretsofdivorce.com

If you're interested in attending a seminar with Christina send and email to: christina@secretsofdivorce.com

If you're interested in teleconferences or group coaching, send an email to: christina@secretsofdivorce.com

This book is dedicated to my father, John Apostol. Although you are no longer here, I continue to feel your guidance and love.

Testimonials

"With Christina Rowe's help and coaching I was able to find a great attorney. I am now able to provide my children with the financial security that they deserve. This book is a must read for any woman going through a divorce"—Cindy, mother of two

"When my ex-husband refused to pay medical expenses for our children, I was able to bring him back to court without paying a lawyer. After reading *Seven Secrets to a Successful Divorce– what every woman needs to know* I was successful in court and saved myself a lot of money in attorney fees"—Sophia Demeson, mother of three

"How I wish I had read this book 5 years ago! I suffered through a long, painful divorce. If the information in this book was available to me back then I would have saved myself money, time and heartache"—Ginny Frederick

"I am currently going through a complicated divorce. I now know how to protect myself financially thanks to this book. If you are going through a divorce I highly recommend you read *Seven Secrets to a Successful Divorce–what every woman needs to know* by Christina Rowe. It is a lifesaver"—Christine Vela

Table of Contents

Acknowledgements

I would like to thank my four wonderful children, Stephanie, Nicholas, Alexander and Sabrina for your love and support. You are my inspiration and I love you more than anything in the world.

To my brother and mother, George and Mary Ann Apostol for everything you have done for me. You both have been there to help me throughout the most difficult times of my life. Your continuing faith in me means more than you know.

Thank you Colleen Flynn-Antonis, Esq. Your kindness and compassion helped me through my darkest hours. I will never forget how you saved me, then a complete stranger, from spending the weekend in the county jail!

To Pasquale Ferro—You stood by me and inspired me to fight when I had given up.

To Denise and Alyce—it is wonderful to have great friends like you on my side.

To Steve Nevins—thanks for being there for me, your support means a lot.

Peter Heyrman—without your guidance this book would have not been completed. Thank you.

Amanda Vas—you have been a truly inspirational coach and I thank you for all of your wisdom.

Roan Kaufman—You have helped me tremendously with this book. Your coaching and great advice has been a godsend.

Hobie and Cathi from Dunn & Associates—Thank you for the wonderful cover design and for being so supportive.

Thanks to Ronnie, my terrific hairstylist and everyone at Vogue Hair and Nails for your support.

Thanks to Fred and Ginny for being so supportive.

Thanks to all of my friends in the "loop" online. Your input on everything from the title to the cover has been a great help.

Introduction

What are the secrets to a successful divorce? Can a divorce ever be considered "successful"?

Five years ago if you told me that I would be divorced today, I wouldn't have believed you. I was completely unprepared for my divorce, both emotionally and financially. How I wish I had had someone to guide me through the trials and tribulations of this unknown territory. At the time, I felt completely lost and unsure about how to handle my divorce, which ultimately consumed a year-and-a-half of my life.

If only I had received some guidance from a mentor, someone to offer the secrets that could have protected me legally and financially, I would have been spared a lot of heartache.

I've written this book so that I can be your mentor today and provide you with a guide to a successful divorce. And yes, keep in mind that you can survive divorce and even become happier than you ever imagined.

In this book I will give you the Seven Secrets to a successful divorce, plus several bonus secrets that you must know. I am going to offer one of those secrets right now, and this secret is the most important one. I want you to keep it foremost in your mind as you read the rest of the book and most importantly as you go through your divorce.

So what is the most crucial secret you need to know to have a successful divorce?

It is the simplest secret, yet the most difficult one to master: Controlling your emotions!

I coach many women who just can't seem to understand and follow this one piece of advice. Usually by the time they come to see me they have made quite a mess of things. I have coached women who have been divorced for years and still can't control their emotions when it comes to their ex-husband!

Granted you are going through one of the most difficult times you will ever face in your life, and so you may feel angry, hurt, sad, and confused.

It will take immense stamina and self-control, but you must get—and keep—control over your emotions. Your ability to do so will affect everything from how you fare financially to how your children adjust.

Losing control and showing emotion is how you lose this war. Do not be fooled, divorce is a war. You need to prepare for battle and master the art of winning the divorce war.

How do you control your emotions when you feel like you just want to scream?

1. Do not speak to your soon-to-be ex-husband unless absolutely necessary. When you do engage in conversation, speak only about your children or other important issues. Control the temptation to tell him that he is an idiot or you hate him! When you feel that you want to say something derogatory, get off the phone or walk away. Remember self-control!

2. Resist the urge to spy on him, ask neighbors and friends about what he is doing, or grill the kids about his girlfriend. I have known women to make prank calls to their husbands, drive by their ex's homes repeatedly, and do other crazy things that were used against them in a courtroom. One woman was actually sued because she wrote a nasty comment about her ex's girlfriend on the Internet. She didn't even refer to this woman by name, but the implication was enough for the judge to give her a guilty verdict and a fine.

3. Do not talk incessantly about your ex. You do need to talk to someone to let out your anger and rage, but limit your circle of listeners to a few good friends and family members. The clerk at the supermarket doesn't need to know just what a bastard your ex-husband is! Anger is like a fire that needs fuel to grow. The more you talk negatively about your ex, the angrier you will become and thus increase the chance of losing your temper.

Overall, think about the outcome you desire. Do you want to have the judge presiding over your divorce respect you, or do you want to look like an angry, bitter wife who is out of control?

Most people lie in family court, which is why judges rely on their own impression of a couple to see if the husband or wife appears more credible. Your behavior outside of the courtroom is crucial. Out-of-control behavior will almost always wind up back in the courtroom and cost you dearly.

So see a therapist, meditate, do whatever it takes to gain self-control. This is imperative at every stage: when you are thinking about getting a divorce, during the process, or even if you are already divorced. Your ex-husband is not going to go away, unfortunately, so you will need to find a way to deal with him in a calm and dignified manner.

I realize that some books on divorce advocate getting revenge on your spouse or using unethical tactics in order to win your divorce case. But I am a firm believer in karma. No matter how despicably your spouse may act, you should never lower yourself to his level. Take the high road. That is not to say that you shouldn't protect yourself, however. The information that I provide in this book is designed to give you the tools you will need to succeed in your divorce. At no time do I advocate that you act in any way to intentionally hurt your spouse.

There are plenty of maneuvers you can employ to outsmart your spouse without resorting to dishonest actions. We will review in detail what you need to know so that you can be fully prepared and protected.

I discuss my personal story in each chapter, hoping that my experience will help you through your personal journey into divorce. My divorce was ugly and bitter; learn from my experiences so that your divorce will be easier. Take what is written here, apply it, and you will master the secrets to a successful divorce!

1

D-I-V-O-R-C-E:
Why We Get Divorced

My marriage ended when my ex-husband had an affair. That incident sparked the fire, but, as with most blazes, there had to be kindling. Our marriage had already hit hard times well before that. The affair may have provoked our divorce, but the split was also the result of what his affair revealed about our marriage.

I hadn't realized how close our marriage was to disaster, and neither had my husband. I had no idea that the glue holding our union together had dissolved so thoroughly. Though I had seen evidence of my husband's infidelity on our computer years before, I closed my eyes to it. For his part, he had no idea that there would be a price to pay for his actions. He had deceived me, but he had also deceived himself into thinking he could get away with almost anything. These misperceptions kept both of us from recognizing that the bonds of our marriage had been disintegrating for a long time.

We were no longer friends. In many ways that loss of friendship was at the root of our divorce.

Many divorce lawyers will tell you that marriages end because of a lack of communication. A famous study in *Cosmopolitan* magazine noted that one way to predict the success of a marriage was to look at each spouse's relationships before the marriage. Did they both have close platonic friendships with members of the opposite sex? If they did, this is a good omen. The point behind this is that so much of marriage is not based in the romantic relationship, but in how two people who live together get along. Romance plays an essential role at pivotal moments, but through most of the hours of the day, spouses deal with the basics. There are meals, bills, and the raising of children. Spouses have to deal with each other's work, hobbies, and personality flaws. They have to figure out when it's time to draw close, and when to give each other room. These are the skills of friendship. A wife and husband had better be friends throughout the day, or there's bound to be trouble.

There are no absolutely reliable figures on how many of us divorce. Several states, including California, don't keep a tally of divorces. That makes any truly nationwide numbers impossible to calculate. Still, a number of organizations and agencies try to figure it out. For many years the U.S. Census Bureau said that 50% of all marriages in the United States ended in divorce. Several years ago the National Center for Health Statistics revised that figure down to 43%. In 2002 the Census Bureau pushed it back up to 50%, but a recent New York Times survey puts the figure at 40%. From these figures it's easy to see that no one knows the exact number, but clearly the fact is that a lot of us divorce.

But why do we divorce?

Because we are no longer friends?

If so, what killed the friendship?

It's easy to say that a marriage failed because of an affair, or a lie, or some other breakdown. But what caused the breakdown? In most divorces there is a trigger, then there are reasons for the trigger, and finally there are underlying causes.

Affairs and abuse can comprise all three factors: trigger, reason, and cause. Most surveys find that affairs and abuse taken together cause 45% to 55% of all divorces. Affairs are usually listed as causing anywhere from 25% to 34% of all divorces. In most polls 15% to 20% of all respondents mention abuse as the main reason for their breakups. Because of the dominance of these factors, we will deal with them in chapters of their own.

In this chapter we will touch on certain situations that might lead to extramarital affairs, or domestic abuse, but we won't go into those two problems themselves.

With that in mind, let's look at just a few of the major factors in divorce.

YOUTH

When two very young people enter into marriage on nothing but a feeling and a whim, their youthful impulse can easily become the trigger, reason, and cause for the breakup, all in one. Sometimes, looking back at such unions, one gets the feeling that the divorce grew directly out of the wedding ceremony. (It's no accident that Nevada is both the wedding and divorce capital of America. To gamblers, everything is temporary.)

Young love has always been regarded as the most fleeting, and statistics confirm this belief. In April 2005, the New York Times reported that 60% of all marriages that end in divorce do so in the first decade. One in 12 marriages end in the first two years. This doesn't count annulments, which are almost as common as divorce in the first couple of months after a wedding. Several studies have shown that the most dangerous years of marriage are the first two, and this is particularly true for people under 30. We have long heard about the "seven-year itch," but it's the two-year itch that should get our attention. This is the expiration date for most lust and infatuation. By this time two people had better be on the road to a real friendship, or they may be headed for a crash.

Most of us have seen this in action. Forced marriages seem particularly susceptible. If pregnancy is the biggest reason two young people marry, divorce is often a short way off.

But just as pregnancy doesn't always lead to an unhappy marriage, postponing children until after marriage is no guarantee of success. Youth itself can be a predictor of divorce. Teen marriages are notorious for their brief duration. If you think back to the first time you felt you were in love, you might see the underlying reasons in your own personal memories. It makes us wonder: if the teenaged Romeo and Juliet had lived, would their marriage have survived with them? If we went by the statistics, we'd be shaking our heads.

Marriage is one of life's great decisions, but when we're young we're making many choices, great and small, that determine so much about our futures. When two teens marry, each spouse agrees to limit their choices to those that will be possible within the confines of their spouse's life. Often it doesn't take long before new choices and desires come into conflict with the marriage vows.

As people age into their late twenties and thirties they become more settled within themselves. Aging can bring the risk of becoming so set in your ways that you can't adapt to another person, but usually that doesn't become a huge problem until middle age. The statistics vary, but most people feel that the optimum marrying years come in a person's twenties or early thirties, when the wild oats have been sown, the passions have settled, and two people are most ready to commit to a successful marriage. Still, as most of us know, even with such optimum conditions, these marriages are far from risk-free.

SEPARATIONS

Any marriage can fail. Marriages among adults can break down because of affairs, conflicts about work, or that catchall excuse: incompatibility. Jobs that involve travel can hurt a marriage, as can any sudden, prolonged absence.

Wars spark divorces as much as any other factors of separation. The "Dear John" letter is a symbol for wartime sadness. In modern wars, with women serving in combat zones, this has been joined by the "Dear Jane" email.

The relationship between war and marital strife has been true since ancient times. Homer's *Odyssey* is about a war-weary husband and the wife and home he left behind. Similar tales persist throughout history, in everything from biblical stories to stories from the Civil War. Some people living today remember the wartime separations of World War II, the Korean War, and the Vietnam War, and most recently the conflict in Iraq. When a husband and wife are apart for six months or a year, the strains can become unbearable. With no partner at home, adultery becomes more of a temptation, and when one person is left with bills, children, and upkeep of the home, it's easy to get angry.

At the same time, the spouse who has left has entered a different world, one where there are no wives or husbands present among their coworkers. Foreign lands present temptations, as does a military where both men and women serve. Though many regulations govern this issue, in war zones, rules are made to be broken. Affairs do occur, some with civilians and others within the ranks. Marital difficulties during wartime may stem from simple absence, or absence compounded by adultery. War was not designed to be easy on marriage.

While war as a cause for divorce is in the news lately, there are many causes of marital conflict whether we are at war or at peace. Family strains can include children, other family members, occupational hazards, and many more.

Jobs are also a source of separation and conflict. Sometimes a job involves a lot of travel. This brings about situations similar to those of military marriages. There are men and women who can make a marriage thrive on such absences, but they are rare. Usually constant or lengthy absences place strains on a marriage.

Jobs closer to home can also make life difficult. A British study by Grant Thornton found that one in sixteen divorces stemmed from one spouse being a workaholic. Even if this spouse works near home, he or she may rarely be present at home. In some ways this situation is more emotionally straining than a spouse who travels thousands of miles away from home. The workaholic spouse may be in an office or other business just a few minutes away, so his or her absence is more clearly a chosen one, implying a rejection of home and family. Often it is just that.

Being a workaholic can be compounded by the temptations of the workplace. Most workplaces have both men and women, and in an office, plant, or store they are separated from home in several ways. Often a person's working colleagues are somewhat or totally separate from the friends one sees at home. There are plenty of instances of office romances that go on for years undetected.

This kind of temptation is more pronounced in certain businesses. People in hospitality trades (hotels, restaurants, and resorts) often stray. These are occupations where being friendly is an essential part of the work. A certain amount of socializing is encouraged. Often if you are friendly, your customers are friendly in return. This can lead to a blurring of the boundaries separating workers from customers. Once again, it becomes easy to shrug and say: "Rules are made to be broken." This is especially true if the ties at home are already fraying.

FAMILY PROBLEMS

Child rearing is often a hidden cause of conflict that spouses only discover once children are born. Surveys indicate that disagreements over treatment of children may be the primary cause of one in ten divorces. A man and woman might talk about how they think children should be raised, but all talk is hypothetical until they actually have children together. Only then will they find out for sure if their approaches are compatible. Often one spouse may be quite lenient in areas where the other is strict to a point that may seem harsh. Many couples can work out such differences through discussion and compromise, but others find attitudes toward children to be a marriage-wrecker. This is an area where marriage counseling can be helpful.

One good piece of advice to unmarried couples that are thinking about taking the big step into having children is to look at the family of your partner. If your partner was raised in a way that is completely outside your experience, talk these matters through. Bring up hypothetical situations, or describe treatment you disagree with, and see what he or she says. If you find your partner agrees with a philosophy toward children that is incompatible with your own, you must consider this as a serious matter. These differences need not reach the level of abuse. There are many ways to raise children.

Differences might stem from religious or cultural conflicts, or simply from personal preference, but they are usually deepseated. Even people with similar attitudes toward child rearing find things to argue about. Totally different methods can lead to war—not a recipe for a happy, healthy marriage.

Other family members can also contribute to divorce. We have all heard too many mother-in-law jokes, but there is a kernel of truth to them. In-laws, whether they are fathers, mothers, sisters, or brothers, often play a role. These people were the primary influences in our spouses' lives as they grew up. That influence may lessen a little in adulthood, but our upbringing is always with us.

Once again, people who are considering marriage should look carefully at the families of their partners. This is not to bring back the old prejudices of class, race, religion, or economic status. Two people can come from very different backgrounds and create a successful marriage. But if there are differences, look closely at how your partner has reacted to them. See if you are on the same page. Of course, if you're already married with kids your options narrow. When this gap can't be bridged, divorce may become inevitable, but even then two people should work toward some kind of accord. Unless one partner is going to be cut completely out of the child-rearing process, the two of you should at least communicate. The emotional health of your children depends on it.

CHANGING LIVES

The Grant Thornton survey listed mid-life crisis as the cause of one out of eight divorces. Though women have more obvious physical symptoms in menopause, male menopause causes more divorces. This is evidenced by the fact that 70% of the divorces among middle-aged couples are brought by wives against their husbands. We've all seen the stereotypical 50-year-old male who suddenly buys a motorcycle or sports car (it's always a challenge to find a leather jacket that fits over a beer belly!).

But sports cars, motorcycles, and leather jackets are the lesser symptoms of a male's change of life. At the same age when they begin to look longingly at a new motorcycle, many men try to recapture their youth with a younger mate. This phenomenon occurs often enough among the more affluent that there is a name for it: "trophy wives." The term demonstrates how much of an insult this practice is to middle-aged women, and to women in general. People aren't meant to be "trophies," and the man who leaves a faithful wife behind should not get a reward. We can't deny that it happens, and the rejected wife who files for divorce has ample reason. We can only hope that justice prevails.

ADDICTIONS

Addictions may be a cause for divorce, and sometimes multiple addictions occur simultaneously. Alcoholism may be present in a marriage where gambling is also a problem. Drug addiction may combine with alcoholism. There are cases where people (mostly men) get addicted to sex. This was the situation in the celebrity divorce between Halle Berry and Eric Benét. Although Berry paid $600 a day to send Benét to a clinic for treatment, the marriage still failed.

Gambling is a classic cause for divorce, with many recorded instances of this problem throughout history. In the nineteenth century, for example, a young groom who lost his fortune betting on horses or cards was a familiar plot in plays and novels. Women were drawn to these stories because the plots reflected their daily lives. Today gambling remains the cause of as many as one in twenty breakups.

TRAGEDY AND DISASTER

Tragedy and disaster can also be implicated in many divorces. Parents who have lost a child run a high risk of breaking up in the first two years afterward. Each is a reminder to the other of the child they created and lost. This loss takes many forms. Sometimes spouses will blame each other for the child's death. Other times they simply don't understand what role the child played in their family. A child can be the glue holding parents together, but often they don't know that until the child is gone. The child dies, and the parents' worlds change radically, carrying them off in different directions. Two people who both understood perfectly why they were together suddenly can't see any reason for living in the same house.

This is particularly true when the death is of an only child. It is also more prevalent among parents of a child who has died from a long lasting, debilitating disease. Such parents have invested so much of their love and hope in the child that death leaves them with nothing. Marriage requires energy and commitment. Parents in this situation often feel as if they've used up all their emotional resources on the child they've lost.

We can see cases of divorce stemming from disaster among the survivors of Hurricane Katrina. When people fled, families often had to break up temporarily. A wife might have gone to her parents, while a husband went to his, or perhaps they simply wound up with two sets of friends 500 miles apart. Even those couples that settled together have found their lives turned upside down. Should they go back to their homes? Do they still have homes? Is there any money left? Is there work wherever they've landed? These uncertainties provoke splits. When couples lose an anchoring family member, the loss only adds fuel to the fire.

OTHER TRIGGERS FOR DIVORCE

Some upheavals are self-imposed. One often cited cause of divorce is home improvement. This may sound like the stuff of a comedy routine, but it's true: many marriages break up during, or after, a major renovation. It isn't so odd when you think about it. Most marriages go through periods of fragility. A woman may feel stifled and claustrophobic. She talks about her feelings with her husband, and they agree that the answer might be a bigger house. Instead of moving, they add on two large rooms. Suddenly they are living in the midst of a construction project. Every day brings unwelcome changes. Workmen invade their house. The place is always dusty and dirty. They have rooms they can't use. For a while the house is smaller, and they both have less space to call their own.

This is when all the weaknesses in a marriage become visible. Tempers are short. Sins, flaws, and imperfections all rise to the surface. One begins to wonder how the marriage survived the first clogged sink or blown circuit breaker.

The events causing a divorce often overlap. We have already seen this overlap in the statistics cited above. For instance, a workaholic husband may also have an affair with a coworker. His working wife comes home night after night to a house where she is left alone to deal with kids, bills, and all the other responsibilities of the marriage. She seldom sees her husband and is already considering a divorce. Then she learns of his affair, and that seals the fate of the marriage.

Or two young people meet, fall in love, and quickly marry. In their first year of marriage both get jobs where they travel a lot. Neither one has an affair, but after several months both are thinking about it. They are in different cities every week, with different coworkers. There are no kids, and to the world each of them looks single. They begin to feel single. At some point they're both back at home for several weeks, and they find that they are nearly strangers to one another. With no children and little property, this couple should be able to make the break more easily than most.

FRIENDSHIP

Even with all these stressors on a marriage, it still comes back to friendship. How do two people feel about each other in the day-to-day sense of living with one another? Romance is fine, and the sex might be great. These are things that can help a marriage past some minor rough spots. But most marriages face a cataclysm or two. It might be a lost home, a lost child, or some form of lost innocence. It might come in a needle or a bottle. A husband might bet the rent money on a losing horse. A wife might find a job that takes her away from home for weeks at a time.

But if two people are truly best friends, they will find a way to treat one another with love and respect. They will appeal to each other's sense of humor. They will know each other's weaknesses, but never attempt to exploit these. The marriage may not be free of trouble or hurt. There may be some jealousy, boredom, and failure. But two people who have a core of real friendship will usually find their way through.

Many divorces result from two people beginning as passionate lovers, but never seeing past this to become caring friends. Others result from a couple being passionate for a while, then friendly for a few years, but never truly forging the real bonds of friendship. In some cases lovers become enemies, split up, and then, after a time, realize they are friends. There might not be any remarriage. Scars may be too deep, they may have remarried, or they may find they only get along when they aren't living in the same house. The variations on these scenarios are numerous.

Whatever the reason for your split, don't expect to be able to see it while you are getting divorced. Others might recognize it, but the divorcing spouses are the last to know. They only want out. The true reasons for divorce are usually only understood in hindsight.

CHAPTER

2

Overcoming Abuse: No More Tears

If you or your children suffer from sustained abuse at the hands of your spouse, this is just cause for separation and divorce. Most studies find that abuse is the major factor in anywhere from 15% to 20% of all divorces. It is a lesser cause in others.

Men cause most abuse, particularly physical abuse. Abuse can come in several forms. The two largest categories are physical and mental abuse, but mental abuse is almost always a part of physical abuse.

Some behavior is only abuse when it occurs again and again. Someone may lose their temper and behave in an inappropriate manner, yet they are not considered to be an abuser. This happens when the person who behaved badly shows genuine remorse *and corrects the behavior.*

To distinguish between real abuse and isolated instances of bad behavior, look at the issue of power. If a person loses his or her temper in a way that gives that person power over you and your actions, and if that person uses that power to deny you freedom of choice, that is abuse.

Physical abuse can pose a clear and present danger to you and your children. If you feel the threat of physical abuse is imminent, and you have no reasonable way of stopping it, then you should take your children and go to a place that is safe.

Abuse was a factor in my own divorce. I go into the details of that experience elsewhere in this book. If you or your children are victims of abuse you should seek help as soon as possible. Never allow an abusive situation to continue. It will only get worse.

THE FIVE TYPES OF ABUSE

Physical abuse is slapping, hitting, pushing, shoving, or any physical action that is calculated to injure, intimidate, or cause pain to the other person. This kind of physical action can also include choking, using an object (cane, bat, kitchen utensil) as a weapon, and holding a person against her will.

Mental abuse is any abuse that is intended to cause mental disorder or derangement, or to impair the judgment of its victim. Mental abuse plays on the victim's emotional weaknesses and frame of mind. It often involves lying and deception. In some instances it is carefully calculated, in other instances the abuser is simply acting as a predator who instinctively recognizes and takes advantage of any weakness.

Emotional abuse often overlaps with mental abuse. This is abuse that plays on the fears and emotional vulnerabilities of the victim. It can take many forms, the simplest being yelling, insults, and threats. It can often involve other friends and family. An abuser might isolate his victim, cutting her off from those who might help her. An abuser might use violence against an animal, or against another person or child, to strike at his intended victim.

Emotional abuse can be far subtler than other kinds of abuse. The outlines are more difficult to see. Most of us yell now and then, and many of us occasionally say things we regret afterward. A true emotional abuser will use this fact to portray his or her behavior as normal and within bounds. An emotional abuser will often try to make a victim feel guilty, manipulating facts and feelings. An emotional abuser will also coerce a victim into saying and doing things she wouldn't say or do otherwise. In this way the abuser puts the victim in a compromised position in terms of friends, family, and children. She apologizes for him, and because she is embarrassed by her own weaknesses, she becomes isolated. Abusers use many forms of coercion and isolation.

Emotional abuse often includes dominating behavior. All decisions are taken out of the victim's hands. This includes even the smallest economic decision, even if the victim is the primary wage earner.

True emotional abuse repeats itself. It may be sustained (repeating constantly in defined cycles) or chronic (erupting now and then), but if it occurs more than once, it will probably continue until someone takes action to stop it.

Sexual abuse is sometimes a part of physical abuse. It involves any unwanted touching of a sexual nature. Sexual abuse can also include demands for unwanted sex, and the use of threats to get sex. It can be used on spouses or children, and is sometimes used on both. Marital rape (sex between spouses where one spouse is not consenting) is a form of sexual abuse. No form of sexual abuse should be tolerated, and any sexual abuse can be a cause for divorce.

Stalking usually occurs after a couple has separated. It includes following the victim through daily travels; making harassing phone calls; monitoring a victim's home, office, or any place where she may be present; confronting or arranging to run into the victim in public places; or constant visits to the victim's place of work.

Abusers of any kind have certain traits in common. Abusers tend to be frustrated in their lives outside the marriage or relationship. These frustrations may stem from work, other social interactions, childhood traumas, or all three. In any abusive situation the abuser seeks confirmation of power and satisfaction of desires.

SITUATIONS AND STATISTICS

Domestic violence and emotional abuse complicate any divorce proceeding. I have seen this, and experienced it myself, in physical, legal, and emotional terms. A spouse can use words or physical actions to threaten something worse. A spouse can use the children, as well as friends and family, to maneuver and weaken a former partner.

In some cases it isn't this subtle. There are marriages that have reached the point where a beaten-and-battered wife must escape, often with her children. This moment might come as a complete surprise to her, or it might be something she has a chance to prepare for.

According to the National Crime Victimization Survey, the number of incidents of domestic violence dropped slightly in the 1990s. In 2001, however, former or current spouses committed 691,710 nonfatal victimizations. In 588,490 cases (85%), the victims were women. These were nonfatal attacks.

In the same time period, intimate partners murdered 1,687 people. Women accounted for 1,247 (74%) of these murder victims. Despite the decline in overall domestic violence, the number of women murdered by male husbands and boyfriends did not go down.

Taken over the last 15 years, the collective statistics show that somewhere between one in five and one in three (20% to 33%) of all women have been victims of some kind of sexual assault or rape in their lifetimes. Many of these occur within a relationship with a husband or boyfriend.

Violence and abuse of men at the hands of women is not unheard of, although physical abuse of men is far less common. Physical abuse of men leads to the suicide of the victim in a much higher proportion than physical abuse of women. There are many theories for this, including a woman's strong protective instinct toward her children and desire to live in order to care for them.

Divorce is not always a solution to domestic violence. Some abusers become more enraged, and return to assault their exes as divorce proceedings go on. Women who are taking flight should do all they can to make certain that they are going to a place that is secure from attack.

The overall rate of domestic violence is certainly higher than shown by the statistics. Many incidents are never reported. Exact figures on how these numbers relate to divorce are also difficult to calculate. No state keeps precise records on this issue.

According to the *Mental Health Journal*:

"The precise incidence of domestic violence in America is difficult to determine for several reasons: it often goes unreported, even on surveys, there is no nationwide organization that gathers information from local police departments about the number of substantiated reports and calls, and there is disagreement about what should be included in the definition of domestic violence."

Abuse is named as a cause in about one out of six divorce actions. Most studies find that about 60% to 65% of the abuse named in divorce action is purely spousal. About a third is child-related, or involves abuse of both spouse and children. A great deal has been made of allegations of abuse that have turned out to be false, but in divorce cases these are in the minority. A study of 215 divorces that included allegations of sexual abuse (of both children and spouses) found that 67% of the allegations were true, 12% were false, and 21% did not involve a spouse. (These last were cases where a step-parent, babysitter, or some other third party was abusing a child, and figured into the divorce proceedings, so the accusations weren't made directly against either spouse.)

HOW TO DEAL WITH ABUSE

Sustained abuse of any kind must be stopped. If you are a victim it is up to you to take the first step. This might involve counseling, but only if your husband goes willingly, and cooperates fully in all strategies and actions aimed at protecting you and your children. Often a realistic program of rehabilitation will involve a period of separation between the abuser and his victims.

If the abuser does not fully cooperate in such a program voluntarily, he will probably continue the abuse. If this happens the abused spouse must prepare to escape from the violence.

HOW TO ESCAPE AN ABUSER

There are many important things you should do if you are an abuse victim preparing to leave your spouse. These include: making copies of important records, papers, and bills; putting these records, some cash, and extra clothes in a safe place or a trusted friend's house; and leaving when you must. If you can, start your own bank account. Get credit cards in your own name.

If the threat of physical violence is imminent, escape with your children as soon as you can.

In such a situation, have an escape plan. Figure out what room in your house is most secure and has a reasonable exit to the outside. Be prepared to give in to verbal demands in order to buy time. Once you have determined that the moment has come, go immediately. If you see a dangerous situation arising, do whatever you must (short of increasing the physical danger to yourself or your children) to create an opportunity for escape.

Once you are away from the home, go to the nearest shelter, or to the home of someone you trust. Also consider whether your spouse will follow, and if so, where he is likely to look.

USING THE LEGAL SYSTEM TO ESCAPE AN ABUSER

As I noted above, often a divorce action provokes an abuser. His violence may escalate. Protective or restraining orders can help, but they can also further infuriate the abusive spouse. Law enforcement can't protect a victim or children around the clock. This is something you should discuss with your attorney.

Remember, when you ask for a protective or restraining order against your spouse, the judge will want as much evidence as possible. Document erratic behavior and any violent actions starting now. You can do this by writing everything down, or keeping a computer file, but be sure it is safe from discovery. Try to recall each detail. Ideally such records should be moved to wherever you are keeping your important papers in case of escape. One way to keep things written down, and retrievable from anywhere, is web-based email, such as yahoo or hotmail, as long as you make sure the password is secure, and that you log off whenever you are finished. You can write things and save them as a draft, and there is no risk of losing the hard drive if you have to leave in a hurry. Call others as soon as possible after an incident, and have them keep a record of it. If you have bruises, show them to others, and ask them to make a written note of what they've seen. Keep the paperwork on hospital visits. If you have made any 911 calls, get the tapes of them. Your attorney will need as much evidence as possible.

If you are representing yourself in a motion for a restraining order, and you have such proof, let the evidence speak for itself. There is nothing wrong with expressing your fears, but do not say more than you have to against your spouse. If there are witnesses to violence, and/or solid physical evidence (cuts, bruises, broken items), these will be the most convincing factors. Most judges will be impressed more by a victim who simply states the need for protection and then presents compelling evidence. If you have a lawyer, but still have to testify, do so without anger. Present yourself as a victim of deranged behavior, and in need of a sane, sensible solution. Concentrate on the violence of the abuse, rather than on the abuser.

Judges seek to be referees in divorce disputes, not favoring either side. A judge will often resent being manipulated into issuing a restraining order early in the proceedings, especially if the victim later uses it as evidence in the divorce trial. Show that your concerns are only for the safety of yourself and those around you. Demonstrate that the order will be a useful tool in cooling things down and producing a just settlement.

Another issue that will concern a judge is the children. Judges are prone to try to sustain contact between parents and children. If your children are subject to abuse, then any protective or restraining order should apply to them. If the abuse is not aimed at them, and you intend to allow your spouse any contact with the children, discuss this with your lawyer. Often a restraining order can be limited in a way that is designed to defuse the anger of the abuser.

There are also other options to protective and restraining orders. In most states, a party in a divorce action can ask that a no-contact order be a condition of the divorce proceedings. However, these usually expire with the final decree.

SETTLEMENTS

The extent of abuse, and the potential for further abuse, should be the most important factors in any settlement. If there is an obvious threat of further abuse to a spouse and/or children, the contact should be limited or completely cut off. The safety of the victims must be the basis for settlement.

If the abuse is confined to the spouse, and isn't sustained or life threatening, a judge will often arrange for visitation rights with the children. If this is the case, make sure all conditions are met to ensure your own safety when exchanging children for a visit. Judges sometimes draw up conditions for these exchanges that include third parties (trusted friends or family members), performing the exchange in a public place, or other security measures.

HEALING THE WOUNDS OF ABUSE

How does one heal oneself or one's children from the traumas of abuse? Physical wounds and scars are problematic enough, but much of the injury is done to the heart and mind. How can a victim become whole again?

The aftereffects of abuse can take many forms, including depression, post-traumatic stress disorder (PTSD, which includes numbness, edginess, and reliving the event), insomnia, headaches, muscle aches, aggressiveness, delinquency and school problems (in children and teens), and withdrawal.

Encourage children and teens to talk about it. You don't have to be pushy, but always let them know you are open to their problems. If problems arise with their teachers, neighbors, or other kids, try to use these as opportunities to get the child to talk.

Remember, many of the same things apply to adults. Depression and PTSD were first recognized as adult problems; however, we now know they have a role in children's lives too. If you have successfully escaped from an abusive situation, and all the evidence tells you that you and your children are reasonably secure, watch out for signs of depression and PTSD. If you find yourself dwelling on what happened, or if you are often overtaken by feelings of fear, malaise, or pessimism, talk it out with someone you trust. Don't be afraid to seek help. There are many counseling programs available through state and local agencies. Don't feel as if you have to tough it out on your own. These problems are real, and can be as debilitating as any physical wounds. If a physical injury continued to bother you, would you hesitate to go for help? Injuries to the mind and spirit are the same.

In divorces that grow out of abusive situations the abuse is almost always the biggest factor. It looms over all other things. Make sure your divorce is a solution to the problem, and not something that will make it worse. It is your job to separate yourself and your children from all violence. Do whatever it takes to further this cause.

CHAPTER

3

Dealing with a Husband Who Cheats

Discovering your husband is having an affair is a shock. Nothing can prepare you for the moment when you realize you are being betrayed. No one has ever betrayed you like this before. Not a friend, family member or even a lover's betrayal can compare. Most divorces involve sharp emotional injuries and an affair is the worst cut of all.

I will never forget the day I realized my husband was cheating. He was having an affair with someone who worked for me. I was stunned. I felt as though I had been stabbed in the stomach. The pain nearly took my breath away. At first I was in a state of shock and went numb. Even though I was faced with overwhelming evidence of my husband's betrayal, I still found it hard to believe.

Day in and day out for those first few months, the thought of them together literally made me ill. My appetite vanished. I had nightmares. In one dream I walked up to my husband, only to find his girlfriend sitting in his lap. Then I would wake to a world where that scenario was real.

In the first months after my discovery, the affair was a day-to-day, moment-to-moment intruder in my life. I couldn't escape the fact that I had been basing my life, my hopes, and my dreams on my husband's lies. In my mind our future had always been one of "we." Now I had to adjust to the idea that he had a different "we" in mind.

In those months I felt a terrible sense of sadness and loss. I also felt angry. I was angry with my husband, but I was even angrier with the other woman. To say I hated her is too mild a description. I felt what any woman feels when her husband betrays her. This woman threatened my home, family, and all the things I had built since my marriage. She threatened the core of my life.

Several weeks after my husband moved out we spoke on the phone. He told me he no longer loved me. That alone hurt enough, but the deepest injury was in his attitude. The man who had lied to me was in love with his mistress. He was also radiantly happy. For him there was no sadness or loss. I couldn't begin to comprehend this. I thought our values and emotions ran on the same track. We'd been married 13 years; we had four children together. How he could turn off his feelings so easily? How could he simply turn away, and immerse himself in this love born of betrayal? I was dealing with a different person now, someone I did not know. The shocking realization that this was a man I had once trusted with my life. This was a man who was by my side as I gave birth to my children. Now my best friend had transformed into my worst enemy.

I was overwhelmed.

Do spouses who cheat care? Do they harden themselves so that they can ignore the pain they're causing? If they could feel the actual pain they are causing would they change? Would they care then?

Most of us who have been the victims of adultery have been forced to ponder these questions. We look at spouses who we lovingly trusted, people with whom we've had children, and we see them walking away, blind to the tears, and deaf to the sobs of others. It is as if they have found a way to separate themselves from all that led up to now, and cut themselves off from the past.

As we ponder, we ask why? A woman asks: was I not good enough? A man might ask: was I not caring enough? Either might want to know: Did I keep up my end? Was I supportive enough? We blame ourselves, and examine every small detail. Like detectives we search for clues, leads, and turning points. We ask the questions of a spouse who is no longer there, and in the end we are left right back where we started: Why? Why would my spouse choose to destroy our marriage?

There are no easy answers, but there are guilty feelings that can and should be dealt with. First, remember: you did nothing to make your spouse stray. This was their choice, freely made. There is always a moment (or moments) when a responsible person can say: No. The responsibility is theirs, and for those of us they abandoned the question is not: Why did my marriage break up? Instead we begin with: did a perfectly loyal, loving spouse really suddenly turn into a cheater? It's likely that the answer is: No. Which leads us to the question: Are there signs that we ignored?

I searched my soul, and my memory, and found that the answer was: Yes. The indications were there, and I ignored them. I had evidence that my husband was not the wonderful, trusting man I had made him out to be. I put on my rose-colored glasses, and saw him only through those lenses, filtering out anything that might threaten my family and me.

After the marriage is over, it's often a good idea to look back and learn. This shouldn't be the kind of thinking that only leads to you torturing yourself. If you're still at that stage, don't dwell on the past. Only do this when you are far enough past the shock and the wreckage that you can think of it as an object lesson, and want to avoid the same traps next time.

When you have reached that stage look carefully, and ask yourself, were there times when your spouse treated you badly? Was there verbal abuse — the kind that builds slowly, so you get used to it, and ignore it? Did your spouse's behavior change at some point? Did odd quirks develop? Did you ever catch your spouse in a lie? Was there flirting with the opposite sex? Sometimes it's useful to list these things, and try to put them in order. What happened when? Did one thing always follow another? Did your spouse always grow cold with you just after flirting with someone else? Or just before? Did your spouse get short-tempered for days after being out late? Remember, behaviors usually have connections. It's up to us to try to see those connections.

Such an examination will almost always reveal one truth: you are not responsible for your spouse's affair. You cannot control another person's decisions. You didn't violate your marriage vows. Your spouse did when he decided to have an affair, and he made that decision again and again, for a long time as the affair went on. A truly noble person who was unhappy in their marriage would stand up and say it was over before engaging in an affair. Cheaters are cowards. There is no excuse and no justification. A truly mature man or woman will face their partner, and end the marriage honestly.

Once you realize this, you will start to regain a sense of peace. It is not within your power or your responsibility to change another person. Only they can change themselves. It is time to rebuild your own sense of worth. You are a strong person. If you weren't, you couldn't deal with such heartache.

This is one of the tests of character we all undergo in divorce, a challenge that should bring out our strengths. Once we reach this point it is time to focus on rebuilding our lives. We must overcome anger and bitterness, heal our wounds, and move on to a positive place. The hurt will not magically go away. But through time, it dulls to a sense of sadness and loss, a scar that serves as a reminder to watch for those signs and clues the next time, and to avoid the pitfalls. As you move on the process will come to feel like the mourning of a loved one, though this person is still alive and, if you have children, is still a presence.

This is where it gets tricky: in the situations where you must still see, or hear from, your ex. In some ways this is harder than mourning. A death freezes someone in time, and we can look back and select what we prefer to remember. With an ex-spouse we don't have that option. There they are, first on the other side of a courtroom, and later picking up the kids or dropping them off. You may both have to be present—possibly even together for some moments—at graduations, funerals, and even weddings and christenings. Such contacts don't allow you to form and preserve your own private image of a person the way death does. If you have a school's invitation to sit near or even next to your ex and watch your child receive a college diploma, you had better deal with your angry thoughts and feelings. You need to reach a level of forgiveness, not for your spouse, but for yourself.

If you harbor anger and resentment for too long it will spill over into every part of your life. Your children will feel it and suffer. Friends and coworkers will sense your bitterness and avoid you. Eventually you will isolate yourself from everyone.

The best revenge is being happy! There is nothing sadder than a person who is still badmouthing an ex-spouse years after the divorce is final. You know the person I'm talking about. You've met her at parties; you've seen her in the supermarket. Every conversation turns into a trial of their ex, with them as prosecutor, and you as judge. They have to persuade you of their point of view. They have to know you're on their side. They won't be happy until you hate their ex as much as they do. And even if you agree with them on everything, the next time you see them they have to convince you again. Time after time they want every friend to pronounce their ex guilty.

You don't need to be this person. You have been betrayed and hurt, but do you want to be alone too? Being a victim of betrayal doesn't mean you can never trust again. You can heal, and come back, carving out a new life for yourself. You can find new loves to talk about. You deserve a life filled with happiness and joy. The road there will be long, but you will eventually understand the past well enough to arrive at a place of peace. But you must overcome bitterness and hate, and replace them with healthy, positive thoughts of good times and a bright future. It may take years to achieve this, but if you are striving for it, and taking real steps toward it, people will see that you're rising up rather than falling. If you keep at it you will learn from the past and take this knowledge into the future. Have faith and be sure that a brand new life awaits you.

In this process the issue of forgiveness is the most challenging. Forgiveness isn't easy. I know of a woman whose husband was taking prescription medication for the herpes virus for a year. He had contracted the virus from his lover. His wife had no idea he was cheating, and so she was shocked when she found a sore of her own. This is how the wounds of betrayal can become physical as well as emotional. There have been cases where the same thing has happened with AIDS. I don't know if any of us can expect a person in such a position to find forgiveness. Fortunately most affairs do not have fatal side effects.

One question we all ask is: Why did it happen? Why would someone do something so hurtful rather than take the route of honesty? In preparation for this book I have done research and interviews, and I've concluded that people who cheat are caught in a sort of limbo. They are looking for something outside the marriage that will ease their boredom, lift their depression, or simply add excitement to their lives. However, most of them are not ready to end their marriage. They are confused, and in their confusion they become selfish. They want to "have their cake and eat it too." Some are convinced that they won't get caught. Others assume that if they are caught their spouse will tolerate their affairs. Some count on forgiveness. Others do consider the possibility of their marriage ending, and simply do it anyway. They give in to immediate temptation, and then find themselves stuck in a web of deceit.

As I've coached women through their divorces, I've heard many stories. One comes from a woman we will call "Nicole." Nicole was celebrating her son's first communion with relatives and friends at a restaurant.

She was in the ladies room when her eight-year-old son burst in and announced to her: "Daddy's gay!"

Nicole laughed at her boy. "That's nice," she said. "I'm glad Daddy's happy." Then she went back to the party, and a moment later she was shattered by the revelation that her husband, after a few too many, had announced he was coming out of the closet and leaving his wife.

Nicole proved that a woman can recover from the harshest shocks. She did divorce her first husband, and is now happily re-married and the proud mother of a baby girl. She is living proof that we can move on.

"Frankie" is a 42-year-old father of two who had been (he thought) happily married for 17 years. Frankie was stunned to learn that his wife was cheating on him with his good friend. Frankie began to break down emotionally. He lost weight, be-came depressed, and even tried suicide. Obsessing over ways to get revenge, he spent two years in chronic pain. His downward spiral showed in his work. It looked as if his last hopes for hap-piness were slipping away.

Then, when it looked as if he was about to hit bottom, some-thing happened. It was as if some missing cog finally fell into place. Frankie realized that he was the source of his pain. Yes, his wife and friend had done him wrong, but now he saw that the torture had long outlasted any injury they could do to him. It was his own inability to let go and move on that was hurting him.

Slowly Frankie took control, one step at a time. He began ex-ercising and eating right. Soon, he started going out with friends on the weekends. He did the things that made him happy, instead of wallowing in sadness. Eventually he met someone. Frankie felt good about himself for the first time in many years.

If your spouse has cheated, you may feel as if your life has no meaning. Depression is very common after trauma. After the shock wears off, and you begin to feel real emotions again, you are the one in the driver's seat. Ultimately you must decide whether you will pull yourself out of it. You create your reality. Are you going to let what has happened to your marriage defeat you or are you going to view this as an opportunity to begin a new life?

I learned of my husband's affair three years ago. Although he still denies it, it no longer matters to me. Still, the memory of that time haunts me. Betrayal does that. But it also did something else for me. It made me stronger. I now see my husband's betrayal as my rebirth. A new me emerged, more confident and secure in the knowledge that I can handle life better than I could before. I can no longer imagine being married to my ex-husband. More than anything I feel pity for him.

The woman he gave up his marriage for, the woman who exposed him for what he was, left him as soon as his money ran out. Her departure was a major relief and we have finally been able to communicate in a civilized manner for the first time in years. He does from time to time revert to his emotional abusive behavior and I quickly refuse to have any contact with him other than email until he treats me with respect again. He has a new girlfriend and things are calmer then before. Although we continue to have moments of discord, I do try and get along with him for the sake of our children.

You might not be so lucky. Your ex may marry the other woman, or simply go from woman to woman, or worse. The circumstances of divorce are seldom easy. It will take soul-searching and acceptance to get beyond betrayal. But if your spouse stays with a new mate, you will need to find some sort of peace with that person, if only for your children's sake. They are what make all the effort worth it.

Affairs are a stunning betrayal of the heart and the pain can cut through you like a knife. Trust me though, if you choose to, you can learn from it and come to realize that you have grown and are a better, wiser, stronger person. Sometimes the most difficult lessons in life are the ones that force us to break out of our box and make a decision. You can either learn from the pain or you can be destroyed by it. Everything depends on where your thoughts are. Control what you think about and you will control your life.

SEVEN SIGNS OF A CHEATING HUSBAND

1. Is your husband suddenly paying more attention to his appearance? Is he wearing new clothes, using cologne, and making sure his hair is combed? If this is not his normal behavior, then this is a huge sign your husband is having an affair.

2. He is critical of you and has been picking fights lately. This is another big sign.

   My ex was very cranky around the time he was cheating. I couldn't understand why he was so angry with me. I remember one night he got dressed, put on his shoes, and brushed his teeth. I thought it was odd because it was late and it looked liked he was going somewhere. Instead he sat on the couch. As I was finishing something on the computer, he yelled, "So you're not going to spend any time with me? Fine, I'm going to my friend's house," and he got up and left. I realized later that he was purposely picking a fight with me so he would have an excuse to leave the house. His "friend," of course, was his lover!

3. Watch out if your ex is suddenly too nice to you. If this not his normal behavior then he could be feeling very guilty and trying to assuage his pangs of guilt.

4. He doesn't want you using his cell phone. This is how my divorce began. My ex twisted my arm when I wouldn't give him back his cell phone. He knew that I would discover the calls to his lover. Ask your husband if you can use his cell. See his reaction.

5. Is he staying up late surfing the Web until the wee hours of the night? He may be having cybersex, looking at pornography, or instant-messaging his lover. If you are computer savvy, you can check your computer and find

out where your husband has been on the Internet. There are also programs you can install on your computer to monitor activity and find out what is really going on.

6. Does your husband have a newfound interest in hanging out with the guys? Did he just start a new hobby or join the gym? Is he gone certain evenings of the week? You may want to discreetly follow him one evening and see where he is really going. My ex started hanging out with one of his buddies several times a week. This was the same guy he would go out with maybe once every few months. It became obvious later that the "buddy" was his girlfriend.

7. Is he no longer interested in having sex with you? Was he always wanting to be with you in the past but now has lost interest? This is another huge sign. Sometimes, though, it can be the opposite: the guilty husband syndrome. He may want to be intimate with you even though he is getting it somewhere else too! I coached a woman who found out that her husband was cheating the morning after he made love to her. Apparently he had been intimate with his mistress the day before too!

CHAPTER

4

What You Must Do Now—Before You Ask for a Divorce

Are you considering divorce? I'm talking about quiet, sober consideration of a question, not the thoughts that flare up from the heated emotions that come right after an argument. Have you thought through the effects of a divorce, and come to the conclusion that you may want to act? If you have, there are things you should do right away.

If your husband has already filed before you, then you must act immediately. If not, you should take certain actions quickly, but not carelessly. The things you do now will affect every decision throughout the process, right down to the final decree.

If you have reached the point where divorce is a clear option, and particularly if you are considering an action that shows that you mean to separate from your spouse (if you are thinking of leaving, or asking him/her to move out), you should do the following *before* approaching your spouse:

SEVEN THINGS YOU MUST DO BEFORE APPROACHING YOUR SPOUSE ABOUT DIVORCE

- Make copies of your spouse's pay stubs for the past eight weeks.

- Make copies of your joint tax returns for the past five years.

- Copy all bank statements and documentation of stock accounts, IRAs, and pension plans.

- Make copies of all of your monthly bills over the past three months. These should include mortgage statements, rent payments, utility bills, car payments, insurance premiums, children's expenses, medical expenses, and credit card statements.

- Copy deeds to any properties owned jointly or in your spouse's name.

- Copy documents relating to any investments. These should include stocks, bonds, real estate, and any corporations or businesses owned in any part by you and your spouse.

- Make a list of all collectibles, jewelry and other valuables. Photograph or videotape these items. Also list all furnishings and take pictures of these also.

> **SECRET #2** • YOU MUST BE PREPARED! THE ACTIONS YOU TAKE OR DO NOT TAKE WILL DIRECTLY INFLUENCE YOUR FINANCIAL OUTCOME. DO NOT BE NAÏVE WHEN IT COMES TO DIVORCE. THIS IS WAR!

This may seem like an overwhelming task, but doing it will ensure that you have all the information ready when you need it most. Once you leave, or if your spouse leaves and takes these records, then you may have to ask your attorney to file a motion to force your spouse to produce them. That would become just another costly hassle down the line. Avoid it. Make copies.

Why do you need all these documents? If divorce proceedings get into a courtroom it means you and your spouse are in a battle. What are at stake are almost certainly income, lifestyle, and assets. You and your spouse are sorting out all of these things in a courtroom, so you need to establish the cost of living and the lifestyle you and your family enjoyed while married. This becomes the baseline the court will use for a settlement. The judge will base decisions about child support and alimony on this information. You must show what your family spends on maintaining a home, food, clothing, transportation, health, education, and any other necessities. In addition, you need to clearly establish what your spouse earns or is capable of earning.

If you exit your home empty-handed, or if your spouse walks off with these records, you have no proof. In theory, the Court can force your spouse to produce these records, but only if your spouse is honest in producing the necessary documents, and only at the cost of one more bill from your attorney. That bill will probably come when you can least afford it. And if your spouse swears that the records produced are the only records in existence, you may be stuck with that answer. Once again: Make copies. Give them to a trusted friend or relative before informing your spouse you want a divorce.

When is it time to make these copies? If, in cool, collected moments, you find yourself thinking of actually picking up the phone to call a lawyer, make copies of these documents first. If you suspect your spouse is thinking of leaving you, make copies. If weeks go by, and you still haven't called the lawyer, but the situation is still getting worse, keep your copies up to date. As the bills come in, copy them, and each month add those copies to the ones you have already given to the trusted friend or relative.

If you do sense that the end of your marriage is nearing, then you should also make financial preparations. If you think there's the slightest chance that a split will turn into a fight (and most do at some point), then it's bound to be more costly than you think. If any part of the settlement winds up in court, your life will be disrupted in ways you can't imagine. Bank accounts could be frozen. Possessions you think of as yours will suddenly be points of contention.

What you need is ready cash. If at all possible, start putting money away. If you have a place to keep it safely, cash is best. But there are other ways of preparing. Think ahead. If you can do it without drawing attention, get the children clothes for the next season or two. Pay fees for their sports and dance lessons ahead of time. Do all this from joint accounts, while saving whatever cash you can on the side. The more you have stashed away, and the less you have to spend during the settlement of the divorce, the better. If your spouse becomes spiteful after the separation, you will have the peace of mind that goes with knowing you took care of the children's needs. That means fewer bills and less stress later on.

The next two steps should be taken only if you are certain the breakup is imminent. If you are about to ask your spouse to move, or if you are the one moving, withdraw half of all funds in all joint savings and checking accounts. These are the accounts that are in both of your names. The court may decide otherwise later, but for now, you are entitled to 50% of what's in them. Take out your money. Leave the remainder for your spouse. While you may be legally entitled to withdraw all of the money in the joint accounts, you should consider what that would look like to the judge who decides your divorce case. If you withdraw only half, you will appear fair, even in the midst of turmoil. Make sure you keep the bank receipts from these transactions. You want to show that what you are taking is exactly half of what's there on the date of the withdrawal.

Next you must cancel all joint credit cards. Also call and remove your spouse as an additional cardholder on any of your own credit cards. This action will, of course, alert your spouse that you are leaving, so it is best to do it immediately before leaving, or just before filing for divorce.

Are these extreme measures? Not if you have already decided to file for divorce. If your spouse decides on a split before you do, you may find yourself presented with a situation where all or most of these things have already been done. You may also find that the arrangements aren't as fair as they should be.

If you think your divorce will be amicable, answer this: have you and your spouse talked about it quietly? Have you each hired an attorney, and selected a neutral mediator to help with the details? If this is not the case, and you have made your decision, and one person's departure from the home is imminent, then you should take these actions. If you don't do it now your attorney will tell you to do it. Your divorce may go smoothly. Unfortunately many divorces turn ugly and you need to protect yourself. Consider this: When my husband was arrested for twisting my arm and threatening me, he used my credit card to pay his bail! He also took our $80,000 in savings and spent it in six months, all while not paying child support.

I had little cash when my husband moved out. I was unprepared. I lived on credit cards. I charged everything from groceries to monthly bills. When I reached my credit limit, I had to borrow money from my family. Let my experience be a lesson.

Make every preparation that is necessary. Do not take anything for granted. You do not know how your spouse is going to react to a divorce.

In the first months after the breakup you'll have huge expenses outside of your normal life. In a contested divorce most attorneys require a $3,000 to $5,000 retainer in advance. Maybe your spouse will be good for his or her fair share of family expenses: housing payments, kids' clothes, utilities, health care, and so on, maybe not. If your spouse does the right thing, your preparations will enable you to deal with any emergencies. But if your spouse walks away from those everyday bills, you still have to pay them. It might take a few weeks or even months to get an initial court date to establish an amount for spousal and child support. In the meantime, you need to be able to maintain your lifestyle and pay your bills.

If you have any reason to believe that the split may involve disputes, you should record conversations with your spouse whenever possible. Certainly this includes phone calls. Some states only allow you to record the person on the other end of the phone line if you have informed them that you are doing so. If this is the case in your state, then always inform your spouse when you turn on the recorder. Make sure your voice is clearly heard at the beginning of the tape, informing your spouse that you are taping the conversation. Your local Radio Shack has recorders that tape phone conversations. Anytime your spouse calls, tape it.

As for meetings in person, carry a small tape recorder in your handbag or strap it to your ankle. This is perfectly legal in many states as long as you are the other person on the tape. If you were to tape two other people engaged in conversation, this might be illegal and considered wiretapping. Check with your lawyer on your own state's laws governing the taping of conversations.

I taped my husband on numerous occasions. My attorney brought the tapes into court. My husband was trying to reduce his support payments by claiming that he could not work in his field because there were no job availabilities. While the recorder was running my husband told me: "Go to hell!" He did so in response to my telling him of a job opening. I also had several recordings of him contradicting himself. In addition I taped him promising to drop several phony criminal charges he'd made against me if I would sign over my interest in our business and a property. In the end he had to drop his false charges anyway, and his threats on tape didn't help him at all.

If you have the remotest reason to think you are in for a fight, get that recorder.

Regarding email communications. Many divorce lawyers will tell you that email can make or break a divorce case. Remember that it is easy in the heat of anger to send an email that you will regret. With a letter, you at least have to put it in an envelope and put a stamp on it. This gives you time to change your mind. With email, once the button is pushed, it's gone, and you can't get it back. Don't send any emails containing threats, emotional diatribes, or profanity. If you need to use email to negotiate things such as child visitation, stick to the facts.

If your spouse makes an email mistake in your favor, don't delete it! Save it, print a copy for your lawyer. It might be the most useful evidence you will ever get. Respond briefly that the accusation is not true, without seeming angry. In some courts, silence in the face of an outrageous accusation might be seen as evidence that the accusation is true.

If your spouse controls your finances, and you do not have access to the checkbook or savings account, this makes things much more difficult, but you can still prepare. Search the house for any hidden bank statements or checkbooks. Once again: make copies.

If you spouse has an account solely in his name and he opened that account during your marriage, chances are you are entitled to half of the funds in it. Exceptions would be inherited monies or earnings prior to the marriage. Even then, if any of these funds were co-mingled, you have a good chance of declaring them marital assets.

You need to do your detective work now. Pay careful attention to your spouse's activities. Look for receipts, and any documents that involve assets or income earned. You need to prove what your spouse is capable of earning. This might be different from what he or she is actually earning right now. Many people are underemployed. If you spouse has degrees and is trained for well-paying work, but refuses jobs in that field, you need to have copies of academic or training degrees or certificates, or previous documentation of his experience and earning potential.

Is your spouse working off the books? This can be a problem. When divorce lawyers know that one or both parties to a divorce work are self-employed, they know they are in for a long and expensive fight to prove income. It is difficult to prove what your spouse is actually earning if he has no pay stubs and doesn't report his income to the IRS. This is where you must gather your evidence before you leave. Get your spouse on tape telling you how much he is making. But if earnings are off the books, consult your attorney. If you have filed joint tax returns in the past, and you knew your spouse was omitting income that should have been taxed, then you too are liable to punishment by the IRS. Be careful! Judges in divorce courts do not often bother calling the IRS when income tax fraud is being committed, but it would certainly not be outside of their rights or power to do so.

Remember: good preparation only increases your chances of a favorable outcome. In court, proof is everything. Do not miss out on money you are legally entitled to because you didn't do your homework.

Some time ago I spoke to a woman who decided to collect all of the paperwork listed here. Although her marriage was unhappy, she thought of gathering all this information as a precaution. She discovered her husband was hiding over $200,000 in stocks. A few months later he asked her for a divorce. He offered her the house and a nice weekly sum for spousal and child support if she agreed to a mediator and did not take him to court. He failed to mention the money in his stock portfolio or the savings accounts he held in his name only. Chances are his wife would have taken his "great deal" without ever knowing about these assets. Now she knows better and is prepared to get what is due to her.

Don't miss a thing. Gather as much evidence as possible. Look everywhere. Use that tape recorder. Unfortunately it's wisest to assume the worst. Once a divorce turns ugly, anything goes. You don't have to push things to extremes, but be prepared to do what's necessary. Protect yourself and your children.

But what do you do if you have very little cash? Make a list of all of the available credit in your name. Check all of your credit cards for the credit limits and how much is owed. You may be surprised at how much open credit you actually have. I was shocked when I found a $10,000 open credit limit on a Visa card I had hardly used. That card put food on the table. When the divorce is final you can liquidate assets and pay these debts, but for now credit is the lifeline of the cash-strapped spouse.

Whatever your situation, stay strong and in control. Protect yourself and your children. Might there be a relative or friend that you could borrow from until the divorce is over? If there are assets, such as equity in the marital home, you might be able to persuade an attorney to hold off on payment until the divorce is final. Lawyers recognize potential assets more readily than most creditors. Also, the court may award attorneys' fees in some jurisdictions, in some cases, and if your attorney is willing to wait, that is more cash in your pocket. However, you should never plan on an award of fees from the court. Remember that ultimately, you may have to pay your lawyer, even if you believed the Court would make your spouse pay your attorneys' fees.

Do not be shy when it comes to asking for help. Being in a tough situation is nothing to be ashamed of. You will be surprised at how people will go out of their way to help you when the chips are down. You just have to ask.

5

Deciding to Divorce

The most intense, heart-wrenching decision comes at the start: Should you get divorced? Much has led up to this question, including the notions of separation and divorce. Up to now they have only been thoughts and words, with no immediate consequences. Now that you realize the time to decide has come, you have to contemplate action. The focus on action clarifies the situation, but also makes it seem more difficult and scary.

Any number of scenarios might lead to the end of a marriage. Sometimes there's no choice; it's your spouse who crosses the line. Often an affair ends a marriage. Other times physical abuse occurs, and the marriage becomes dangerous and intolerable. Circumstances like these leave us with little choice in the matter. A divorce becomes the only acceptable step.

But many divorces arise out of situations that are far less cut-and-dried. You may find that your marriage has grown dull. You look at your mate and realize that all the physical attraction you felt is gone. Or maybe the emptiness is in a different area. You might feel restricted, and even suffocated in everything you do. Your soul mate is no longer your soul mate. Your lives have grown apart. In situations like these others may still see your marriage as ideal, but deep down you feel it is all pain and misery. This may be one-sided. One partner may think everything is fine, while the other only wants out. Or you may be gasping for breath, and not even knowing it. If you come to the realization that your marriage is failing, should you get a divorce?

Before you take any steps you should contemplate where they might lead. Divorce is a painful, difficult choice. Ending a marriage is almost never easy, even when both sides agree that they no longer love each other. When one spouse still has deep feelings and the other doesn't, or when there is any sense of imbalance at all—whether it be emotional, financial, or professional—that can only make it worse. In most cases you are ending a long relationship. There was love here once, and intensity. You are considering cutting the cord with someone who was the most important person in your life.

The presence of children amplifies the problem. The younger the kids, the worse it can be. Most children cannot help but feel torn when parents separate.

Divorce is often a financial earthquake for both parties. The family home might be sold. Two households are set up, both having to accommodate the children. Unless both parties are rich, this will affect your family's standard of living.

Whether the problem is mental, spiritual, or a combination of factors, divorce is a step you should examine carefully. If there is no physical abuse in the picture, you may want to go to couple's counseling before making the final decision. Offer to go with your spouse to see a therapist. Put it in positive terms, and make it a wholehearted offer. If you don't think of it this way, counseling will have little chance of having any value. Your spouse might say no, but you will have tried.

If there is abuse, either physical or mental, couple's counseling is almost certainly not the right course. Spousal or child abuse should not be tolerated. If it happens you need to protect yourself. In such a case you should simply look for the quickest, safest way out. Appeal to friends and family or, if necessary, go to a shelter. Do whatever you must do to effectively separate yourself and your children from your spouse, then look for a lawyer.

Has your spouse cheated? For me this was the cause of my divorce. Some will be able to forgive their spouse and try to save the marriage. I was unable to accept my husband's affair and he quickly changed into a different person, both emotionally and physically, leaving me no choice but to file for divorce.

I know from my own experience and from observation of many divorces, that your road ahead is long, frustrating, and probably ugly. The best scenario would be that you and your spouse begin by meeting with a mediator to agree on a fair settlement. If this route is possible it will save both of you thousands in legal fees. If you feel that your spouse will agree to an amicable divorce, this is the way to go.

THE NINE QUESTIONS YOU MUST EXAMINE IN MEDIATION

1. Custody.

   Care of the children is your most important concern. If custody is shared, what are the terms? If it is not, what is the visitation schedule for the non-custodial parent? Don't forget holidays and summer vacations.

2. Housing.

   Who will retain the family home? Will the martial home be sold and equity split equally? Or will one party keep the house and buy the other out? (In my own divorce I kept the family home. I waived alimony payments in exchange for equity in my home. Alimony is taxable, but the equity in your home is not, so keep this option in mind.)

3. Alimony and child support.

   How much will go to whom?

4. Tuition.

   Who will pay for school tuition? Will he pay for private or public universities? Might issues regarding paying for tuition become an issue later? Don't rely on oral promises, "Of course I will pay for college!" is often said at mediation but not committed to writing. Unfortunately, in most jurisdictions, once a child is 18, there is nothing the Court can do to force a parent to pay for college.

5. Division of stocks, bonds and other investments.

   What is the proper division/liquidation of stocks, bonds, bank accounts, and other holdings and investments? What about the 401K plans, retirement funds, and life insurance? How will this be divided? A minimum amount of life insurance should be a provision of every divorce settlement, without exception.

6. Marital debt.

   Who borrowed what? Who charged what?

7. Determination of incomes.

   Who made more money? Who contributed what, and what are the values of those contributions?

8. Wills.

   Will you have wills drawn naming the children as the beneficiaries?

9. Health insurance.

   How will health insurance be addressed?

If you are going into mediation, remember that every aspect of your financial life with your spouse has to be closely scrutinized. These will be weighed in terms of your lifestyle and your standards of living, both together and apart. You will need to itemize all household expenses, household contents, properties, bank accounts, retirement plans, vehicles, furniture, and other items of value. Make sure you take into account all childcare costs, including daycare, religious education, sports, and other after-school activities and lessons. Consider the cost of birthday parties attended, lunch money, school dues, clothing, and camp. If your children are young, adjust for expenses as they grow, and include those projections in your plan.

It's best for you and your spouse to gather all of this information beforehand; doing this together can be useful. If you find yourselves disagreeing on something, set it aside. Agree to bring up all disputes only when you are with the mediator. If you can do this, then mediation might be the route for you. If you have problems with your spouse while gathering information, it may be a sign of bad times ahead.

If you and your spouse can agree on a fair settlement and iron out the details of your divorce without bitterness you will be extremely fortunate. Your children will be spared any emotional trauma and you can co-parent them together. This is an ideal situation, and if you are lucky enough to have a cooperating spouse you will emerge from your divorce as unscathed as possible.

This usually isn't the case. Often the subject of mediation doesn't even come up. If the decision to divorce is one that is forced on you, and you are placed in a role of opposition from the start, there's really no decision at all. Then you must prepare for war. In this case you must simply gather all of your resources: those within yourself, as well as the support of your family and friends.

At that point the decision transforms. There is no choice in your divorce. The only decisions lie in the matter of how to divorce. Now you must protect yourself and your children legally and financially. You need to find an attorney and prepare for battle. The actions you take now will affect everything you do later.

The path of divorce is not an easy one. Think it out carefully, and never go into it lightly. If this is the path you choose, do not be naïve, and protect yourself at all costs.

CHAPTER

6

Secret Tips on Finding
the Right Attorney

Finding the right attorney can be a daunting task. Most of us have heard jokes portraying lawyers as money-hungry sharks. Unfortunately many of these jokes are based on truth. As you begin this journey, your choice of a divorce attorney is among the most important—a make-or-break decision. You must be careful, for some lawyers specializing in divorce will purposely prolong proceedings for financial gain. Look before you leap.

When I first realized that I needed an attorney I had no idea how to find one. I went to the Yellow Pages and picked one out. I hired this lawyer to handle a court date concerning my restraining order against my husband. I wanted the order made permanent. The proceedings were held before a judge, with testimony and other procedures working much as they do in a trial. My lawyer (we'll call him "Tom") saw the opposing attorney and immediately went on the defensive. A municipal court judge from a neighboring town was representing my husband. Apparently there was a problem between these two attorneys, and Tom was sure we would lose.

I felt the facts were on our side. My husband had twisted my arm and threatened my life; I had a police report and a doctor's note. Yet these facts hardly mattered to Tom. There was my husband's attorney, and with him was the police officer who took my report at the station.

"This looks bad," Tom told me.

"How can that be?" I asked.

"He's got the cop on his side," said Tom. "I don't see how we can win this."

"I can't believe that," I said.

"But it's true," Tom said. "I think we're beaten on this one."

I might have given up right then, but the next thing I knew the judge was allowing me to testify. I told the judge my story. The police officer helped my case, admitting that I appeared to be in pain at the time. The judge granted a final restraining order. I paid Tom $1,500 for nothing more than being a scared rabbit. I knew I didn't need that kind of representation, so I went looking for a new lawyer.

This time I asked around, searching for referrals from people who had gone through a divorce. My father helped me, finding a firm that came highly recommended. One should remember that while a law firm may have a good reputation, every lawyer is different. Each firm has lawyers who are better at some things than other things. Some law firms are only loose cost-sharing arrangements, and the "partners" do not keep track of the quality of work produced by the others. Talent and experience vary from one lawyer to the next.

In my case, the attorney my father had heard about was on vacation. They asked if I would care to see another lawyer in the firm. I agreed, thinking: if it's a good firm, then all of these people must know what they're doing. This became my second mistake.

The lawyer we'll call "Cathy" was in her late twenties. She exuded a professional air as she advised me on strategy and the nuts-and-bolts of filing divorce papers. I felt comfortable with Cathy, but my father was disappointed. He wanted the older, more experienced lawyer he'd heard about.

Meanwhile my husband had taken some actions of his own. He'd filed for his own restraining order against me, claiming that I had threatened him in a parking lot in front of my children, my brother, and his mother. He also claimed that I hit the window of his van while trying to punch him. He had a scheduled visitation with our children at a restaurant. Both his attorney and mine had spoken the previous day and Cathy advised me that I would be receiving a child support check from my husband.

When I approached him to ask if he had the check, he ignored me and rolled up his car window. I had a few unpleasant words with his mother and then walked away since my children and brother where sitting in my car only feet away. So when I got notice to appear in court, I wasn't worried. My children and my brother would testify that this simply did not happen. I felt sure that when we got to court, this case would be thrown out.

Once we were in the courtroom my husband's attorney had a chance to show his stuff. He was loud, manipulative, and scary. He yelled at the witnesses and spoke so quickly that it was difficult to answer. Once I saw the way he worked over witnesses I decided against putting any of my children on the stand. I didn't want them to have to testify against their father. My brother was my witness and my husband's mother was his.

The problem came when Cathy proved to be just as intimidated by my husband's attorney as Tom was. In the face of his onslaughts she froze. Cathy began to stutter and could barely cross-examine a witness. She didn't ask my husband more than two questions before resting her case. She was clearly nervous and in over her head. I was shocked.

Suddenly there was the judge issuing a restraining order against me. The judge explained that he did not find any of the testimony from either side credible and he did not believe I threatened or tried to hit my husband. He did however site a law that implied that if I had any contact with my husband's car that was enough to order the restraining order against me. Since a restraining order was issued against my husband, when I approached his car I essentially forced him to violate the restraining order.

I sat there in disbelief. The only contact I could have with my husband would be phone calls to discuss the children and our business. I was quite upset with Cathy. I called for a meeting with the senior attorneys in the firm. Cathy was removed from the case and I got a new attorney, Ryan. Ryan didn't come free. I had to pay $5,000 immediately. (This was in addition to the $5,500 I'd already paid this firm, which was gone in six weeks.)

I thought I was at rock bottom, but there was still some downhill left. My husband had supervised visitation at the courthouse every weekend. I was to bring the children there by 9 a.m. One Sunday shortly after the restraining order was issued, I called my husband to ask him if he was going to go to the visitation since it was snowing and the roads were icy. I left this message on his cell phone and he did not return my phone call. According to both restraining orders, contact was allowed only to discuss the kids or the business. Several days later, while I was at work, the police arrived. They had a warrant for my arrest. I asked them what on earth had I done? It was surreal. I had not been anywhere near my husband, had not spoken to him, had no contact whatsoever.

The warrant stated that my husband claimed that I had called him several times and emailed him. That was it. Now I was being arrested for something I hadn't done. The judge who had signed the warrant wasn't local. He was from the town where my husband's attorney just happened to be a judge himself!

They took me out to the police car in front of my employees. My panic was nearing hysteria. I called my lawyer. Though I hadn't yet paid the new retainer I felt sure he would do something. The people at his firm said they would work on getting me out. They never called back.

My warrant stated, "No bail." This was just after 4 p.m. on a Friday afternoon. All of the judges had left for the weekend. I was in for a stay at the county prison. First they would send me to the police station in the town where the judge had signed the warrant. From there I would be transported to the county lockup. I called my parents, sobbing. I asked them to go get my children, fearing that Social Services would come for them if no one was there.

Then came a glimmer of hope. One of my employees called her former divorce attorney and explained the situation. This attorney, who I shall call "Darlene," called me at the police station. She said she would see what she could do. As the hours passed, I became increasingly distraught. I cried uncontrollably, and felt faint and dizzy. My blood pressure shot up to 160/100. I wanted to go to the hospital. I was hyperventilating and couldn't breathe. They brought in the Emergency Medical Services. I was given an oxygen mask.

There would be no hospital for me. Once you are in such a situation there is no way to draw the line between yourself and any criminal they might haul in. The police put me in handcuffs in back of a police car, and drove me to the police station in the town where the judge had issued the order for my arrest. On the way I felt wave after wave of nausea. I told the officer I thought I was going to throw up. He told me if I did I would clean it up.

At the new police station, I was fingerprinted and they took my mug shot. As I sat there handcuffed to a bench, I started to accept the fact that I was going to prison. But I had an ally I hadn't counted on. Darlene was an attorney who cared. She spent the entire evening contacting judges, working on getting me bail. She was dogged, and didn't give up until she had succeeded. I will never forget her kindness and what she did for me.

With bail set at $1,000, I was freed. My father came to get me and I ran crying into his arms. I hugged him like I had when I was little. Any differences we'd ever had were gone. He'd rescued me.

This shows how far things can go. When you start down the road of divorce, keep this part of my story in mind. Most people involved in divorce don't go to jail, but it's not uncommon. When it happens it is usually the result of one of two things: a lawyer who doesn't tell you what you need to know, or a client who doesn't listen.

That Monday I called Darlene and set up an appointment to see her the following day. She warned me that my husband could pull this again. He needed no proof. All he had to do was say he saw me near him or that I contacted him, and I would be arrested again. She warned that the second time I would spend an automatic 30 days in jail.

I panicked. When I told my father he was furious. After 13 years of marriage and four children, how could my husband do this to me? I hired Darlene as my new attorney, paying her a $5,000 retainer from my credit card. Finally I had a good attorney who was willing to tell me what I needed to know.

This story would be bad enough if it ended here, but the most tragic twist came last. None of us can see the future, especially when bad is about to turn worse. Later that night, I spoke with my Dad. He was still fuming about what had happened. Just hours later I was at the mall trying to finish some Christmas shopping when I got a phone call from my brother. My father had been rushed to the hospital. He was in the ICU, on a respirator. I hurried to his bedside. He'd had a heart attack. He was only 59 years old. He lay with his eyes wide open and staring. Machines breathed for him, and controlled all of his bodily functions.

I told myself that he could get better. I spent the night with my mother and brother, all of us praying by his side. I told him that he couldn't leave me now, not with everything that was happening. I told him I needed him. I ignored the sinking feeling that he was already gone.

By morning there was nothing left but machine functions. The doctor told us my father was brain dead. He would never recover. We had to make a decision to remove life support. We took a few moments with him before doing that. I whispered to him: "Dad, go to the light. Be with your mother and father." Each of us held his hand. We didn't have to pull the plug. He died there with us.

I blamed my husband. After going from jail, to my father's arms, to his hospital bed, I couldn't help it. I knew that my husband had always disliked my father. The false arrest had put my Dad under extreme stress.

Once again there is a lesson here: a contested divorce, like any conflict, takes a path all its own. The stresses and strains often lead to dark places no one wants to go. This is when you need the right attorney. This is when you need the steadying hand on your shoulder, and the voice in your ear saying: "Sit down. Collect yourself." This is the moment when you need a lawyer you can trust. In a moment when all of life seems to spiral out of control you want the luxury of not having to rely completely on yourself. A good attorney is a shielding presence who will reassure you while giving you good advice.

I spent the next few weeks in shock. Each day was a blur. But that didn't stop the divorce. Three weeks after my father's death, we were back in a courtroom. The divorce proceedings began. Thankfully I now had a good attorney.

The judge ordered us to both drop our restraining orders. He then put us back together at our business, a hair and nail salon, arranging for us to go in on alternate days. The judge set amounts for my husband to pay in spousal and child support. He set a date for us to be back in court to continue the proceedings.

I still had legal problems. I had used balance transfer checks from credit cards to pay my first and second attorneys. Now my husband filed a police report claiming that I had stolen his credit cards to pay my lawyers. The case went to the prosecutor's office. They set a date to present evidence to the grand jury. All this happened without anyone checking to see if I was a legally authorized user of these credit cards. I had the credit card company call the prosecutor. He dropped the case.

The battle grew uglier. Our salon business became a nightmare. Our employees were caught in the crossfire. My husband had many of them sign notarized statements against me. He told them that if he weren't running the salon I would ruin it. The same employees then signed statements for me saying that they had signed my husband's documents under duress, and that I was a good boss. My husband accused me of stealing money. I would arrive at work and he would call the police. It was a fiasco.

I never went near him without a tape recorder. One was always in my handbag or strapped to my leg. I taped all phone conversations. He offered to drop all of his criminal charges against me if I would sign over the business to him. His girlfriend followed me to a friend's business and started taking pictures of me. I confronted her and she started screaming that I was trying to kill her! She sped off in her car, nearly running me over.

She headed straight to the police station and tried to file a report against me. I was lucky enough to have a witness.

In all of this my husband was creating his own troubles, and making my case for me. Although he had not paid child support for months and was now over $6,000 in arrears, he bought his girlfriend a pedigree puppy for $1,000. With limousine rides to New York and a lot of spending on his new love, he was forgetting his children.

This is when Darlene was a godsend, guiding me through every step. She filed the proper motions and helped me endure the court dates. When the judge granted my husband's request that our house be sold, Darlene had the motion overturned. She brought forth evidence and finally the judge saw the truth, and had my husband arrested. The judge set bail for the child support my husband owed. Within hours my husband's girlfriend brought the full amount to the courthouse. The judge also barred him from the salon and put me in charge of it.

Darlene was tough and knew the law. She did not allow my husband to get away with anything. Although the divorce dragged on for ten more months, she didn't waver. I could count on her. She gave me the strength to get through this horrible time.

Be careful in your selection of an attorney. You need to trust your instincts. Ask key questions. What is the minimum retainer required? How much do they charge per hour? Hourly rates are not always so important, however. A lawyer who charges $150.00 per hour might send you a bill for an hour for filing discovery requests and the lawyer who charges $250.00 per hour might bill you for half an hour for the same work. He may be more efficient with his time than the less expensive lawyer or he may be just more honest. Then again, the more expensive lawyer might tell you the job took two hours – the point is not that more expensive lawyers ultimately cost less – it is that you can't always tell by the hourly rate what the charges will ultimately be.

Always ask for referrals. Unfortunately, especially in small towns, having good connections do matter. A lawyer who is either politically well connected, or simply well known and liked by the judges, is sometimes a big advantage. You will sometimes feel as though the judges forget that the lawyers are representing clients and are only deciding which lawyer they like better. Many judges, for some reason, seem to believe the clients of the lawyers they know. It doesn't make sense, but some judges seem to think that the respectable lawyers have respectable clients.

You need to interview people you know who have gone through a divorce. Consider what you hear. Did someone go through hell because they had a bad lawyer, or did a good lawyer help them through a hell that could've been a lot worse? Did another person's divorce go smoothly only because there was little to contest, or did the lawyer successfully foresee problems, and settle them in advance? You may want to find someone who was in a situation similar to mine, where an attorney walked into a mess and guided the client out of it. Can this lawyer avoid crises? Can this lawyer handle crises?

It is also crucial that your personalities click. You will spend a lot of time with this person; you need to feel comfortable with him or her. In the end, consider all these factors, and allow your intuition some sway. Can you get along with this person? Do you trust them?

With your attorney's guidance you can work together and speed the process of your divorce. Once you find the right attorney, you will feel more confident in the outcome.

FIVE TIPS ON WORKING SUCCESSFULLY WITH YOUR LAWYER

1. Beware of an attorney who takes a smaller retainer but doesn't file motions. Some spouses wait for months on end to get court orders for spousal and child support because their attorneys did not file the necessary motions.

2. Remember that when you speak to your attorney on the phone you are being charged per minute. Don't make the mistake of chatting on and on. Get to the point and use a timer. If it is a routine question, such as the date of a hearing, speak with the support staff rather than the attorney. Time for support staff is often not billed, and if it is the fee is at a much lower rate than an attorney.

3. Follow your attorney's advice to the letter. These people go to law school; they should know what they are doing. Making stupid mistakes, like calling your spouse repeat-

edly, picking fights, and not protecting yourself, can lead to bills, violence, and restraining orders. You should limit all contact with your spouse. Only discuss your children and any business you may have together. Let the lawyers do the talking for you whenever possible. That's what they are paid for.

4. Follow the law. The most important thing you can have is self-control. There will be times when you want to act out, call your spouse names, or be vengeful. These actions can only land you in hot water. Taking your spouse's credit card on a shopping spree can give you legal troubles you simply do not need.

5. You have hired an attorney to protect you legally. That attorney is also a huge expense and you want to keep track of what you are being charged. Keep a log of every meeting, phone call, and their durations. Also it is a good idea to record in a journal any incidents with your spouse, so that it will be easier to recall the details in court later on.

Most of all, know that although this is one of the most painful times of your life, you will survive. Finding the right attorney will give you confidence in your case. Your attorney is working for you and together you can plan for and obtain the best possible outcome.

7

How to Win in the Courtroom

The first step to winning in the courtroom is defining exactly what your goals are. What do you want to win? Your lawyer should go through this with you, helping you see what the options are, but ultimately you must choose your goals. Your criteria will depend on your situation: what there is in the marriage. If you have children still living at home, then your first concern is obvious. Their lives and their upbringing are the future, and these must be protected. Other issues will be in the realm of money and property: the house, any assets, and the requirements of a fair support ruling. You must look at these issues before you set foot in the courtroom, and frame your strategy according to your goals. If your divorce is going into an actual trial then you are at war. It is a war you can win as long as you are well prepared and do your homework.

PREPARE FOR BATTLE

In a courtroom battle you have to be ready for your spouse's offense. What will the opposing attorney throw at you? If you are asking for support, the job of your spouse's attorney is to reduce what you ask for as much as possible. The attorney will explain all the reasons that your husband can no longer afford to maintain you and your children in your present lifestyle. None of this will be new to the judge. He or she has heard all these reasons before.

Still, you must support your position. This is where careful planning comes into play. Have your husband's pay stubs ready so you can prove how much he earns. You will want a complete list of assets and their values, as well as debts, mortgages, and any other obligations. You must show the needs of you and your children, and prove your spouse's ability to pay. Then you must be prepared for gambits like the health card.

Health is one of the most common grounds of defense. My husband claimed he was disabled from panic attacks and could no longer work as a network analyst. He claimed that running our business was the only job he could perform. It was less stressful, he said. A psychiatrist had written a letter supporting his contention. This psychiatrist backed up my husband's claim that working in the social environment of our salon was good for his mental health, but that work in the computer field was disabling.

I countered with information I'd gathered from various Web-sites on the Internet proving that running your own business is far more stressful than working for someone else. I introduced business magazines listing "network analyst" as one of the top ten jobs one can find, and I also had articles describing the stresses of running a business. With the help of this information, the judge saw right through his antics.

THE KEY TO WINNING IN COURT: ANTICIPATE AND PREPARE

The rule to remember is: Anticipate and prepare. Think about what your opponent (your spouse) wants, and what he or she will do to get it. Consider their possible defenses and offenses, and then do your homework. Find information to counter what they have to say. Look on the Internet, go to the library, and find magazines and books. When you fight back you need to always back yourself up with proof. Anybody can say anything, but having facts in print is imperative.

All of this must be in the context of the law, and the law can be a brutal thing. The first time you enter a court you may feel overwhelmed. The judge's rulings may seem unfair to the point of being ridiculous. Here is an example: your ex isn't paying any child support and you receive a shutoff notice for the electricity in midwinter. You don't have a court date for another three weeks. Your attorney informs you that you must wait until your court date to get any help. Emergency orders are rarely granted. So your electricity can be shut off while you wait for your court date. You wait, hoping they won't shut it off before the court date. Then, with two days to go, your lawyer calls. Your court date has been postponed! This happens all the time. The calendars of family courts are always overcrowded. You may sit waiting through a whole day, paying your lawyer more with each hour that passes, only to be told that your case has been delayed for two weeks.

Your lawyer will know these things, but don't rely too completely on that. A good lawyer is an expert, but a lawyer is also your representative and your advisor. He or she is there to convey your case to the court. To do the job well a lawyer must know exactly what you are after. But you must have some knowledge of the law as well. Only then can you ask the right questions, and make informed choices when the lawyer presents you with options and decisions. It's essential for you to learn as much as you can about the family laws in your state. These are the laws governing marriage, children, common assets, and divorce.

Every day women suffer travesties of injustice in courtrooms. It is a bruising process. Realize that from the start. Form a thick skin. If you don't, you will be constantly frustrated and upset. I shed many a tear from frustration as my husband walked away without paying our children a dime. At each juncture I returned to a home where every responsibility was mine. I still thank God I had a family that helped me through those dark days. I often think of the women who do not have such support, and wonder how they manage.

Once again, the rule is: Anticipate and prepare. If you realize the road will be a long and hard one, you can anticipate the difficulties, and prepare with the support of your family.

GETTING READY FOR COURT

The process may vary depending upon what state you are in but it generally will go something like this: on your first court date you will be assigned a judge who will preside over your case. At this preliminary conference the judge will consult with both attorneys, and set deadlines for each stage of the divorce. The court will look at the information gathered by both sides, and the legal process of the divorce will begin. At this time the judge will probably set amounts of child and spousal support. These are the amounts your spouse is to pay from now until the divorce is final. This is often referred to as *pendente lite* (pronounced "pendentay leetay") support, meaning "pending decision." Although these amounts aren't automatically those that you will receive once the divorce is final, they are crucial in their importance. Whatever the judge says now will set an informal precedent for what happens later. You want these amounts to be at or above your final goal.

Make sure that the court directs your spouse to send these payments to your local child support enforcement agency. They will forward the payments to you, and keep track of what is owed. Always go through this agency. Although they may be slow with enforcement, they have the ability to garnish your spouses' wages and bank accounts and enforce bench warrants. If your spouse falls behind in payments you will be able to utilize this agency instead of having to pay your attorney to enforce support collection. Some states, however, will not permit this arrangement unless there is a history of non-payment, preferring to let the parties handle it themselves.

As in any court trial, divorce will have a discovery phase. In a divorce this is when each party is required to disclose proof of all finances. You will also have to answer the Interrogatories. This is a long questionnaire asking for detailed information about your finances and other marital issues. These will identify issues of disagreement that must be brought before the judge.

The more problems you need the judge to fix, the more court dates you will have to attend. Every time you go to court you pile up legal fees. I was in court more times than I can remember. Most of my motions were to enforce the support order. Issues involving the business and the children's well being were also addressed. Because my husband was uncooperative and had a devious attorney, my legal fees topped $40,000. My ex was in arrears with his child support so often that he was arrested twice. The second time he spent one month in the county jail.

I was lucky enough to have a judge who saw the truth and believed in putting delinquent parents in jail for nonpayment. Some judges are not as tough. Your spouse might mount up tens of thousands of dollars in back child support before the judge takes serious action. Often a judge will allow your spouse to pay what's owed in small installments added to the regular payments, rather than in an immediate lump sum. You may go for months without support, borrowing from family or maxing out credit cards. You may find yourself getting tiny payments when you were expecting the whole amount.

Any of these outcomes can disrupt, and even devastate your finances, so you must plan ahead. Don't rely on your attorney or the court system for a fair settlement or regular payments. You must be proactive.

YOUR APPEARANCE AND DEMEANOR IN COURT

It's up to you to fix both innocence and guilt. You must be able to do what's necessary to prove your case to the court. It's the judge's job to find out who's the good guy and who's the bad guy. Your job is to prove that you are the good guy and that your spouse is the bad guy. From the moment you walk into the courtroom you must look, act, and speak as the victim. After all, if you weren't the victim, and your ex is a really nice guy, you'd have settled your case out of court. Up to now you should have been nice too, so if you're in a courtroom looking up at the judge that means your spouse is the one who is playing dirty.

So how do you present your case?

WHY APPEARANCES COUNT

First of all, remember that appearances count. The judge probably doesn't know you, so you will be making a first impression. Dress appropriately for court. That means dress with care and respect, as you would for a business lunch with a group of conservative professional people (such as clergymen or school-teachers). No jeans, nothing sexy or provocative, and no garish makeup. Certainly hide any tattoos or piercing. Wear your hair in a simple, neat style. You want to look sensible and responsible.

The same should be true of how you act. Remember what your mother said, and mind your manners. You should do this in any public part of the courthouse. The only place where you might have an excuse to let go is if there is a private, sealed-off room where you meet with your attorney. Otherwise remain quiet and calm at all times while in the courthouse. Don't allow clerks, officers, or anyone else there to witness arguments, shouting matches, or anything more than quiet civilities between you and your spouse. Remember that sometimes the judge's clerk has a lot of influence on the final decision. Don't think that because the judge is out of the room that nobody is watching you and it doesn't matter anymore. It's best to have no contact with the opposition at all. Contact is the job of your attorney.

HOW TO DEAL WITH EMOTIONAL TURMOIL IN THE COURTROOM

Carry this calm behavior into the courtroom. Let your lawyer take the lead. Keep your mouth shut! Your attorney speaks for you here, and you should remain silent unless your attorney, or the judge, directs you to speak. When the judge speaks, pay attention. He is the one who decides things, so he is the most important person there. Don't whisper in your attorney's ear. If you do whisper, remember that sometimes the microphones at the table are very sensitive, and what you say may be recorded by the courtroom audiotape, and heard by the Court Reporter, even if nobody else hears you. You may take notes while the judge is speaking, and if you need to you may show these to your attorney, but wait until the judge has finished speaking. This won't be easy.

At times you'll feel ready to burst. At times you'll feel angry, and there will be moments when you'll want to cry. Someone may say something that begs for sarcastic reaction. Pretend you don't hear. If your attorney is saying something that's incorrect, or if you feel he or she needs clarification on a point, that's what your notepad is for.

To the judge you want to look sympathetic, yet intelligent, confident, and secure. Do not twirl your hair, play with your keys, or fix your makeup. Sit upright, and pay attention to every word that is being said. Your future is at stake. Do not look at your ex or his attorney. If your ex takes the stand, remain calm. This may be the most difficult thing for you. He may lie. He may twist every situation. At the very least he will have a view of the situation that is totally opposed to yours. That's why you are here. Don't lash out. Don't lose your temper. Outbursts are not allowed in the courtroom. You must remain composed at all times. And above all, do not make funny faces or expressions of disbelief. Even if they are genuine, the judge may think you are play-acting, and won't appreciate it. Your future, and that of your children, depends on how you control your behavior in the courtroom.

There is one exception; if you absolutely must cry, do it. Try not to sob uncontrollably, but if something truly devastating occurs, let yourself weep. During a court proceeding early into my divorce, my ex filed a motion to sell our house. The judge granted the motion. I sat stunned. I wasn't angry; I was just very sad. I bowed my head and softly wept. A courtroom can be a quiet place, and it is never so quiet as when someone is shedding heartfelt tears.

If an unpleasant ruling stands at the end of a session, you should consult with your lawyer for a strategy to reverse it later. Sometimes a matter can be negotiated. Other times it must be argued. Argument is your attorney's task, not yours. In the case of our home, my attorney pulled up Supreme Court rulings concerning the forced sale of a home during divorce. She discovered a ruling overthrowing a similar decision that ordered that a home be sold.

At our next court date the judge was surprised at this research, but he reversed himself. He knew that his ruling would probably be overturned, and no judge wants a reversal from above. But he probably also recalled my tears. Remember, judges are human too. If something happens in court and you feel the need to cry, do so. Just do it quietly without fanfare or drama. The subtlety of true emotion is a powerful thing. So you see, do not panic. It's not over until the divorce is final.

In the courtroom good manners remain the rule from beginning to end. When a proceeding has come to an end, always say, "Thank you, your honor," before exiting. Do this every time, whether you have agreed with the court's rulings or not. Any judge will feel more sympathetic to a polite litigant. If there are going to be any discourteous notes sounded in the courtroom, let them come from your spouse.

At the same time, be prepared for your spouse to be at his or her best as well. Your spouse also has a lawyer, and if that lawyer is sharp, he or she will smooth over a client's rough edges. My ex always came to court dressed in a suit and tie, though he rarely ever wore one in everyday life. This can backfire. A husband who refuses to pay his child support, but who shows up in court in an expensive suit, may cause himself problems.

That brings us to another point, one where events outside the court affect the proceedings. There is no hiding it. Actions speak louder than words. When those actions affect children, judges sit up and pay attention. If a spouse is reneging on child support the judge will look askance at expensive clothes, jewelry, and sometimes even a spouse's car. Most judges understand that their first duty in a divorce is to make sure the children are treated as fairly as possible.

BE PREPARED

Whatever the situation, whatever is at stake, remember: be prepared! Be prepared for lies, deceptions, and manipulations. Be ready to be accused of being a terrible spouse and parent. Be ready for unfair rulings, and testimony that brings out a part of the truth, but not all of it. Listen, but don't react. Don't get mad; get justice.

Another thing to recall is that your moments in court are just that: moments. You will have hours and days to recover and to prepare for your rebuttal. Whatever comes out in court goes into the record. Your spouse's motions are there, and you may have the ammunition to counter every falsehood that's recorded. Go home. Read the record. Look at what your spouse has entered into the official record, and then see what you have to fight back with.

I would go home, and find blatant lies in my husband's motions. His accusations crossed the line into total fantasy. Outrage would explode from within me. I would get angry, calm myself down, then I would get really upset, and finally I would spring into action. I knew my case against him, but I worked late into the nights developing my evidence. I would then weave this into a rebuttal. Once I had it all in a concise, well-formulated package, I would take it to my attorney. She took it and formed it into a legal strategy for the next session.

I knew that the judge would hear both of our motions. I had to make it crystal clear that I was telling the truth. I didn't trash my ex, nor did I make anything up. I knew the truth would suffice. The more truth I told, the better my case would be.

There were small, simple things, like his two-pack-a-day smoking habit. There went $50 per week, yet he wasn't paying to support his own children. The judge took it especially amiss when he learned that my husband had bought his girlfriend a $1,000 pedigree puppy, yet couldn't provide for his children.

USING YOUR EX'S BAD HABITS IN COURT

Make a list of all of your spouse's bad habits. Is there gambling? Smoking? Drugs? Liquor? Some amusements, like strip clubs and porn, can eat up the biggest paycheck. Keep your ears open. Friends, relatives, and even your children may spill the beans about your ex. You have to be alert, but be careful of letting yourself go too far with this. Don't sink to the level of the dirt you're searching for. Don't grill the kids about daddy, and don't shatter good friendships, or alienate those who truly love you. If your kids innocently mention something worthwhile, make a record of it. If a friend volunteers information, or if you want to ask for it in an honest manner, get everything you can. But hold on to your own integrity. Don't deceive.

As you gather your information, weave all of your spouse's bad behaviors into your motions. Expose everything in a way that shows the necessary connections. But also, don't go overboard here either: if he is paying his support and you are primarily fighting about assets, do not tell the judge he goes to go-go bars!

There is no reason to intentionally hurt your spouse. You need only prove the points necessary to your case. If he is not paying his support then the judge needs to know what he is doing with his money. If he is getting more than his fair share of assets the judge needs a clear picture of what assets you each have, and who has what claims.

Always remember that what you put out in public can always come back at you. If you are going to use your divorce as a tool to get even, only heartache can come to you. What goes around comes around.

HOW TO WRITE A MOTION

You will be able to save yourself thousands of dollars in attorney's fees by helping your lawyer prepare your motions. Remember, the more work you do, the less you have to pay your lawyer. Current divorce attorney rates range form $240 to $500 an hour, and this is not unusual for a large metropolitan area. You pay for the expertise, but sometimes you wind up paying the same rate for things they pass off to their clerks. You have the information, and as you go forward you'll have a better idea of what you want the law to do. If you do the research, write the motion, and then give it to your attorney to review and edit, you'll save money and time. Also, you can often focus more clearly on each goal. Some attorneys, as a matter of professional pride, professional paycheck or both, will not necessarily appreciate you taking it upon yourself to write the motions. Remember to consult with your attorney before deciding that it will be done this way. However, if you do it this way, after your divorce is final, if your ex falls behind on support payments, or you need to modify support or visitation, you will be able to write a motion on your own and not have to pay your attorney.

A motion is a presentation to the court, arguing for a certain action on a point. Anyone can write a motion and be granted a court date. Representing yourself in court is more difficult, and almost always inadvisable. The old expression "Only a fool represents himself" is true. Judges prefer to hear arguments from attorneys. If your ex has a lawyer you will be at a clear disadvantage.

However, a motion to be heard in court is different. For this all you have to do is go to your local family court and fill out a form asking for a court date to hear your "motion." You write your request on the form they provide. Then it's best to attach a detailed, typed letter explaining the situation, and what action you are requesting.

If your ex files a motion, you will need to respond. You will have a certain amount of days (determined by your local family court) to respond. If you insert your information in the following template, you will have a professional motion to present to the court.

If you are responding to your husband's motion then you are writing a Cross-motion. Make sure to put "PLAINTIFF'S REPLY CERTIFICATION" under "CIVIL ACTION" on the top. When writing your motion, be sure to answer each of you spouse's accusations, in order. (*See following page for a sample motion.*)

To learn about your state's divorce laws, go online. Divorcenet.com is a good source of information. Also your state's court system may have an online source of forms, along with an explanation of procedures and a list of sources for legal assistance.

Much information has been presented here. The process can be overwhelming. Don't let it awe you. Others have gone through it and come out winners. Take your time, learn as much as you can, and whenever you feel totally confused, stop and take a break.

The best advice for winning in the courtroom is to keep cool and have a level head. This is not an easy process, but you will triumph. The court system can work for you. If you keep cool, and provide all the information possible in a sensible way, the judge will see an intelligent, reasonable person protecting a family. No matter how trying the courtroom may become, remember

Your Attorney's Name
Address
Phone number
Attorney for Plaintiff

YOUR NAME: _____

Plaintiff,

Vs.

YOUR SPOUSE'S NAME: _____

Defendant.

SUPERIOR COURT OF (STATE)
COURT DIVISION (NAME)
COUNTY

DOCKET NO.:

CIVIL ACTION

(Your name) certifies as follows:
1. I am the plaintiff in the above matter and I make this Certification to:

> *Here you will write here what you are asking the court to do. Number each request and write it in paragraph form. Also, if you have any documents to submit to the court, list them as exhibits A, B, C, and so on. Make sure to attach any supporting evidence you have in these exhibits.*

> *Make sure you keep your motion simple and to the point. Absolutely no mudslinging! Do not refer to your spouse in derogatory terms and do not ramble on about his actions. Keep to the dry facts. Present them in clear, unbiased language. Your judge will read this, so be professional as possible, while presenting yourself in a positive light. In some states it will be necessary to have this document notarized before submitting to the court. Check with the court for the deadline for motions to be submitted. You must send a copy to your spouse's attorney, as well. But if he does not have an attorney, send it to your spouse via certified mail.*

> *Most Motions of this sort will include a certification or oath. The form will vary from state to state, but an example follows:*

I hereby certify that the following statements made by me in this certification are true. I am aware that if any of the foregoing statements made by me in this Certification are willfully false, I am subject to punishment.

Dated: _____

Your Name: _____

there will be a day when you will go to court and your divorce will be done. You will receive a Final Divorce Order, putting an end to this long battle. On that day you will celebrate your success and emerge into your new life, stronger and wiser!

8

The Check's in the Mail: How to Cope with a Deadbeat Ex

What do you do when your former spouse refuses to pay child support? You've both gone into court. An impartial judge has looked at the situation, and decided upon an amount. It's been put into writing, and your spouse has agreed (no matter how reluctantly). You leave the courtroom sincerely hoping that, with this matter settled, your children are a little more safe and secure. Then the first week arrives. No check. Two weeks go by, and nothing has come. Maybe something does come the third or fourth week, but it is only a single week's payment or a partial payment.

What's the solution? You need this money, as do your children. This isn't some huge cash reward. The judge determines the amount based on the incomes of both parents. Other factors, such as property, tuition, visitation rights, and so on, are taken into account. This is the money for your children's most basic needs. The main criteria are usually the necessities: food and shelter. Clothing, lunch money, sports, birthday parties, and gifts are the extras that most of us have to figure out on our own.

If you are fortunate to have a spouse that pays for the children's "extras," that's great. But what if your spouse won't even come up with the funds to cover the basics for your child?

I've been down this road to the point where my ex-husband was arrested twice for nonpayment. The second time he spent a month in jail. This was not a pleasant experience, and though I'm not going to pretend that I was happy with my ex that day, seeing him taken to the jail in handcuffs gave me little satisfaction. For one thing, it didn't pay for the roof over our heads, or the food on the table. Also, what woman wants her children's father to be revealed as being so irresponsible that he would accept a jail cell as an alternative to making every effort to support his kids?

Jail is the last resort. In my ex-husband's case he'd fallen over $7,000 behind. Every effort had been made to coerce him into compliance. My lawyer, the court, and the whole justice system had run out of patience. He went to the county prison. There he was locked in a cell. Among his cellmates were thugs, junkies, and pimps. This was no country club.

I felt sick to my stomach knowing the father of my children was behind bars. Though he had put me through torture, and had ignored the needs of his children, a month in jail was a fate I wouldn't wish on my worst enemy. How does a mother explain to her children that their daddy is in prison? How do you explain the reason?

This isn't something anyone can hide from them. Your children can sense the problem building. They hear both parents, and both sets of friends, talk about it. Even if you don't discuss these things with them it comes through in sudden bursts of exasperation, and overheard conversations, and in the fact that at some point they simply have less than they had before. Then comes the day of jail. You might not want to tell them, but this event can't be hidden for long.

Children attach their own emotionally scarring logic to it. Daddy was in jail for not paying support for them. So logic says that they are the reason Daddy is in jail. Children end up feeling responsible.

For me that day was hardly the end of it. Two weeks after my ex's arrest, they brought him back to court for review. The judge asked my attorney what we wanted to do.

My attorney said to me: "Do you want the state to continue holding your husband in jail?"

I sat, staring at my husband, his hands cuffed behind his back. He looked disheveled. In his eyes was anger. I held the key to his freedom, and everyone there knew it. In my heart I longed to set him free. But there was also $7,000 that my family desperately needed. At home the pile of bills was growing. There were foreclosure notices on our home and shutoff notices from the power and phone companies. I had nothing to pay them with, and my husband refused to give any guarantees. I was living off my credit cards. I knew that if they let him off, that pile of bills would grow, and soon my children and I would be out on the street. He had already demonstrated that he didn't care. He's spent two weeks in prison showing how little he cared. Also, I was sure he could pay most of the money if he wanted to. It was the combination of all those factors that dictated my decision.

"Send him back to jail," I said to my lawyer. I wanted to cry. I hated the situation. I felt as if I were being pulled into a black hole. Then I thought of my kids. That was what got me through.

Two weeks later, he was released and within days he paid almost $5,000. He did it by selling the family car, and paying me my half. This violated the judge's order that no marital assets be disposed of until a final divorce order was issued, but at least I got some money. The bills, which were fast reaching a critical point, were paid down to where I had some breathing room.

In the end the solution with my ex-husband was the same as it is with many spouses who have problems with support payments: the money is taken out of his paychecks, and I now receive child support on a regular basis. Some of the bitterness has faded, lowering the level of hostility between us. With that settled, our job of co-parenting has become much easier.

Many disagreements over child support never reach this point. Often a spouse simply drags his feet, sending partial payments, missing a week here or there, and the friction settles in like a low-wattage current, making every meeting and every phone call a little more difficult. Often it is these cases that are the hardest. The amount owed mounts up so gradually that you feel drained of the energy to act. But at some point you must. Acting is never easy, but you must remember: the law is on your side.

Is your spouse paying support directly to you? If so, then you should change this arrangement. A spouse who tends to fall behind should have to pay the support to the state agency that handles such things. In my state it's the New Jersey Child Support Program. In your state it may go under another name, but every state has this service. This agency will keep track of all payments and what is still owed. Not only can they collect child support on your behalf, but if your spouse falls behind they can employ enforcement strategies. If your spouse gets a paycheck they can garnish the wages. If your spouse owns property they can put a lien on it, and they can do the same with other personal assets. They can take your spouse's tax refund, or withdraw funds from bank accounts. They can even have a warrant issued for arrest for nonpayment. Once they receive the funds they send them to you, at no charge.

This doesn't solve everything. Like any government agency, this one can be slow to act. But they do have the tools to collect, and eventually they use them. You can obtain the phone numbers for the agency in your state by going to:
www.acf.dhhs.gov/programs/cse/fct/fctz.htm

> SECRET #6 • YOU MUST BE PROACTIVE WHEN DEALING WITH A
> DEADBEAT DAD. THE COURT IS OVERWHELMED WITH SUPPORT ORDERS
> THAT ARE IN ARREARS. WHAT MAKES THE DIFFERENCE IS YOUR
> PERSISTENCE. DO NOT GIVE UP. CALL YOUR CHILD SUPPORT AGENCY
> REPEATEDLY UNTIL THEY TAKE ACTION. KEEP YOUR EYES AND EARS OPEN
> AND PROVIDE THEM WITH ANY INFORMATION CONCERNING YOUR CASE.

THE THREE BASIC WAYS STATES DETERMINE CHILD SUPPORT

In 1998 Congress passed the Family Support Act. This law created guidelines for child support and established three basic ways for states to determine decisions in this area. The first is the Income Shares Model. This provides for payment of sums equal to what the parents would have spent on the child if they had remained married, dividing the burden in proportion to each parent's income.

The second model is based on a percentage of income. This can be set as a flat rate, or a sliding rate, and is assessed on the non-custodial parent's paycheck.

The third method, which is called the Melson formula, sets the level of support payments by looking at the standard of living at the time of the divorce, and figuring what each parent needs for themselves, then taking the children's basic needs into consideration. As in the first model, this method splits the final amounts between the parents in proportion to their incomes.

Sometimes state agencies drag their feet, and other times they simply can't get the money. An ex-spouse may find ways to work under the table, or may disappear completely. If you are owed back support, and your state's child support enforcement agency is not pursuing your ex, and you cannot find out where he works or he is working off the books, then you need to take action.

A little detective work is in order. If you still know people who keep up with your ex, see if you can get one to tell you whom he works for. Where is the job? Can you get pictures of him working? Private investigators cost money, but if you were to hire one, these would be the first questions: Where does he work? When does he work there? How much does he make? Hire the investigator for as limited a job as possible. Once the investigator finds out where the job is, you or a friend may be able to do the rest.

There are online "detective agencies" that claim they can give access to bank accounts, whereabouts, and other information. I have tried a few. The results weren't great. Remember: you can do a lot of investigating on your own and save yourself money. Keep your ears open. Mutual friends and family members are great sources of information. People love to talk. Once they are talking freely they often slip up. As with any other part of this process, this is not something where you want to use your children. However, don't close your ears to what children say. If you find out key information simply make sure you can explain how you got it in some other way. Often if you simply confirm what you know through others, this can serve as your source. You don't want to involve your children in any more conflict than you have to, and you don't want your ex blaming them for something they may not have intended to do.

Deadbeat parents learn many tricks. One is to hide assets by putting them in the name of a girlfriend, new spouse, or parent. That way there is no bank account. Wages (particularly off-the-books payments) go straight into this other person's bank account. Property is in another name. Your ex may even move to another state. The traveling deadbeat is the hardest one to catch.

In any of these situations you will need hard evidence in the courtroom. Hiring a private investigator may become a necessity. There comes a point where unless you come upon a lucky lead, you will need the skills of a professional. As long as you pick the right detective, and know what you want, your money will be well spent. There are also private agencies that are devoted to support enforcement. These agencies work on a contingency fee, meaning they do not charge you unless they are successful at collecting your support. They do take a percentage of the support collected. Do your homework and be careful when selecting a service like this. Find people who have used them. Call or email these people, and ask them questions about their experience. These groups can be useful, but, as with any support agency, the more you understand about your needs and their services, the better they will do. If you go online and look up "Child Support Enforcement" on yahoo.com or google.com, you will find several agencies to choose from.

A court will usually assume that your ex-spouse's income is that which he was earning after taxes prior to the divorce. But what if your ex was working off the books? What if he hardly paid any taxes? This is something you will have to deal with early in the divorce process, when the judge is determining support levels to be maintained during the actual settlement. If you have a spouse who is making a good living, but paying little or nothing in taxes, you must discuss this with your lawyer. It may be impossible to deal with this directly in court without shutting off your spouse's income, or greatly reducing what he gets. In such a circumstance you may want to look into alternatives, such as large cash or property settlements, if they are possible.

If your spouse is still working, but is suddenly making much less at the moment of your divorce, make sure your lawyer knows this and, if necessary, points it out. At any point in the divorce, or post-decree proceedings, a judge will become suspicious of someone who was making a decent living prior to a divorce and is suddenly broke.

Another problem comes with "disability." Many men develop disabilities the moment they see support payments ahead. Don't stand for it. Again, unless they can bring in a doctor and prove their disability, this won't fly in the courtroom.

Almost all of the spouses who are owed support in the United States are women. The Federal Office of Child Support Preliminary Statistics for 2004 reported that over *$107 billion* (up from $100 billion in 2002) was due to be paid for *17 million* children in the United States. The government child support agency collection rate (the percentage of cases receiving one or more payments) was 50%, down from 68% in 2002.

Note these additional facts:

- 50% of all white children growing up in single parent households who do not receive child support live at or below the poverty level.

- 60% of all Hispanic children growing up in single parent households live at or below the poverty level.

- 70% of all black children growing up in single parent households live at or below the poverty level.

- Receipt of child support is associated with significantly higher expenditures on children than from any other source of income.

- Children who receive child support are likely to remain in school, have higher grades and test scores, and have fewer behavioral problems.

The Federal Office of Child Support Enforcement annually compiles statistics from the 50 states and territories. The following table lists state-by-state results for 2004.

State	Number of Children	Total Amount of Child Support Due	Collection Rate
Alabama	230,644	$2,499,632,027	50%
Alaska	49,682	$610,503,044	67%
Arizona	271,280	$2,043,831,587	39%
Arkansas	140,793	$754,154,762	59%
California	1,999,958	$19,311,918,483	44%
Colorado	150,616	$1,218,145,835	41%
Connecticut	200,788	$1,609,329,430	41%
Delaware	62,158	$254,060,301	49%
District of Columbia	98,054	$385,427,656	19%
Florida	810,814	$4,450,725,914	58%
Georgia	477,164	$3,153,110,463	42%
Guam	17,152	$98,686,387	58%
Hawaii	98,542	$592,384,830	31%
Idaho	105,478	$429,401,984	52%
Illinois	741,787	$2,793,325,607	32%
Indiana	353,847	$3,845,966,209	47%
Iowa	173,074	$1,071,650,175	78%
Kansas	142,008	$608,113,770	52%
Kentucky	322,568	$1,534,286,555	45%
Louisiana	303,306	$1,002,954,973	46%
Maine	69,059	$485,693,215	63%
Maryland	279,603	$1,567,171,221	54%
Massachusetts	273,598	$2,107,502,531	45%
Michigan	1,032,947	$8,972,572,657	42%
Minnesota	276,222	$1,566,019,740	64%
Mississippi	348,518	$812,377,470	37%
Missouri	382,074	$2,130,116,426	46%
Montana	41,884	$198,205,637	61%
Nebraska	111,393	$613,690,261	62%
Nevada	131,394	$923,619,653	54%
New Hampshire	44,194	$198,474,226	71%
New Jersey	357,924	$2,457,510,568	64%
New Mexico	82,531	$651,006,235	36%

State	Number of Children	Total Amount of Child Support Due	Collection Rate
New York	993,479	$3,999,544,112	51%
North Carolina	435,755	$1,735,238,083	64%
North Dakota	35,055	$166,101,123	59%
Ohio	1,011,119	$4,441,084,369	55%
Oklahoma	166,043	$919,090,608	49%
Oregon	272,160	$1,252,318,706	46%
Pennsylvania	751,910	$2,253,818,736	74%
Puerto Rico	276,598	$1,013,819,674	42%
Rhode Island	77,373	$190,954,666	30%
South Carolina	245,559	$1,185,268,288	45%
South Dakota	32,088	$139,664,806	55%
Tennessee	373,077	$1,943,718,443	46%
Texas	1,104,413	$8,977,955,095	63%
Utah	94,367	$342,017,300	78%
Vermont	27,547	$105,511,904	72%
Virgin Islands	11,580	$55,202,566	34%
Virginia	356,886	$2,194,136,831	59%
Washington	354,902	$1,972,615,096	73%
West Virginia	114,436	$841,158,565	57%
Wisconsin	346,504	$2,217,595,126	65%
Wyoming	27,790	$230,594,597	63%
TOTAL	**17,289,695**	**$107,128,978,526**	**51%**

More than once this problem has been called an epidemic. This epidemic takes its toll on every victim materially and emotionally. Each of us must deal with it as effectively as we can.

Some deadbeats subvert the system with technicalities. One woman who we'll call "Angela" is currently owed over $10,000 in back child support. She has been to court several times with no results. One day her ex-husband approached the bench and claimed he did not receive notification of the court date by certified mail. This was enough that the judge adjourned that day's proceedings, even though the ex-husband was right there, present. Why would he have been there if he didn't know the date?

Angela's next few court dates were adjourned due to over-scheduling of cases. Still her ex-husband didn't pay. Finally the judge ordered a warrant for his arrest. This is when her ex hired an attorney and contested the amount of back child support. He managed to get the arrest warrant vacated. He was able to pay an attorney but wouldn't pay his children. At this writing another court date is pending. One hopes justice will be done. Meanwhile, Angela struggles to survive and keep her children fed, clothed, and sheltered.

"Debra" is due over $100,000 in back child support. Her ex-husband moved to Texas shortly after her divorce. This is where state lines become an issue. Certain states don't enforce child support regulations as well as others. However, there is more to this story. Debra hasn't done all she can to investigate and force her ex-husband to pay. Because she hasn't used every tool at her disposal we can only guess whether she could get some, or all, of the money. Debra's case is an object lesson. In this battle there are no rewards for complacency.

Let's not be too hard on Debra. Each court date and each decision in the process takes an emotional toll. This debilitation can often become a physical drain as well. The cost of chasing a deadbeat is paid in more than money. While you need to do all you can to get support for your children, you must also temper your efforts with an attitude of peace and acceptance.

If you have done all you can, exhausting every avenue, it may be time to let go. At such a point you must use that energy to accent the positives in your life. You may find that the time spent on pursuit is better spent on furthering yourself and your career. That's not to say that you should ever let a deadbeat ex off the hook. But you can't allow the battle to destroy you either.

I have learned all of this the hard way. Though my ex-husband now pays his child support, I have come to see that I will always have to be the chief breadwinner for my family. I realize now that ultimately the only person I can rely on is myself. With that in mind, I work on my career and focus on improving myself. That way I will always be able to provide the income that my kids need and deserve.

In any future fight I would not allow myself to fall victim to the emotional devastation I felt the first time. My energy now is devoted to positive thoughts and outcomes. I am a true believer in "what you think about, is what you get." I choose to surround myself with positive people and things and have had great results from doing so. Money flows easier to those who have positive energy. Things go smoother, and you feel happier. Never let your ex-spouse's actions affect your peace and happiness. It is just not worth it.

CHAPTER

9

Mourning the Death of Your Marriage

Once upon a time you were married. You shared your bed, your home, and your life with another person. You confided in your spouse, believing with all your heart that the two of you would be together forever. You had hopes and dreams together, plans for the future. You were happy. You were in love.

Years passed. There were fights, but you always worked through them. Did you ever imagine that someday the marriage would end? Could you see it coming? Maybe you could, or maybe not. Either way, it's over. Your spouse, your partner, and the one who was once your friend, is gone. In some ways it doesn't matter whether the marriage seemed mostly good or bad; you will mourn. That's how loss is.

For some the mourning may be overshadowed with relief. If the last years of the marriage were bad, relief is normal and healthy. Nonetheless, the finality of divorce can't come without some sense of sadness. These were vows you took, and you believed what you were saying. No one gets married with the thought that they will ever get divorced. It's something that happens to "other people." I remember not understanding how divorcing couples could get so vicious with one another. I thought that if a marriage had to end, the spouses should be civil and split everything equally.

I couldn't conceive of divorce, much less a bitter, expensive war. How on earth could someone I thought of as my best friend be the person on the opposing side of a nasty court battle?

Can anyone explain all that happens when a marriage ends badly? Probably not. But if the split turns sour (and many splits are fights from the start) it is as though you no longer know your spouse. Your lover and best friend now wants to destroy you. The pain is indescribable. You ask yourself: Did I ever really know this person? Was I only seeing what I wanted to see?

In the course of the divorce proceedings your emotions will run the gamut, from elation to sorrow, from freedom to loss. It shouldn't last forever. Eventually you will reach the point of dealing with the loss of your marriage. You need to mourn it, as you would a death.

I didn't really feel the loss until after my divorce was final. While the battle raged on, I was diverted by feelings of anger and betrayal. I was consumed with getting a fair settlement so I could support my children financially.

Then the divorce was finalized. Only then did I feel the deepest pain and emptiness. I panicked. Even after all the months, and the final decree, I could not believe that my marriage was really over. I didn't want him back. I knew that having him out of my life was the best thing. Yet there was a huge place that remained empty. I was in mourning.

In my mind I was still supposed to be married, my kids were still supposed to have two parents living in a happy home. I wanted to go back to the days when we could always work it out. I couldn't face the truth. My husband had cheated. It had probably been going on for longer than I cared to admit. That fact spelled the end of our marriage. I had to accept that.

There are wives who forgive their husband's infidelity. This was something I could not do. Still, I tortured myself long after making this decision, and long after the legalities were settled. Had I done the right thing? After pain, hurt, and heartache, the suffering of our kids, and the upheaval within our family, was it worth it? Ultimately all these things put an end to a marriage that had come to rest on a foundation of lies. Whatever was ahead would be built on truth. That made it worth it. But that's not clear when you are in mourning.

Now I can say yes, the enormous pain was worth it. It took that much pain to end a life of deception. You can never run away from yourself. Eventually what you know deep in your gut, and in your heart, cannot be denied. I knew that my husband was not the person I had thought he was. Yet I had lived with the lie for years. Now it's over and I feel free.

Even now the pain still lingers in my soul. We will never be the same family again. The trust is gone forever. Christmas, other holidays, and the way we experience our children are not the same. I accept that now. Through the loss I can see that most of the changes in my life are for the better.

Recognizing and accepting pain is what mourning is all about. It is a path through the ruins. Feeling bad never feels right, but sometimes it is necessary. Bringing yourself to want a divorce is never easy, but if it's going to lead to something better, you must come to grips with it, both at the start, and even more after the battle is over. Remember you are dealing with a death. Time heals all wounds, but painful times never pass soon enough. Even after years a little ache lingers. That is the scar tissue. It is the reminder of the end of your dreams.

You can begin to deal with mourning if you realize that when one door closes another opens. It's time for you to go through that next door and see what lies ahead. That's not to say that you should walk into just anyone's arms and fall in love again. Be careful, and do not settle for less than the very best. We all deserve to be loved. We deserve to enjoy a relationship based on trust and understanding. Be sure you know what you are looking for; be sure you see it. You may have to wait quite awhile before you find that someone special. It is worth the wait.

The time you spend on yourself will be well worth it. This period after divorce can be a wonderful catalyst for a new and exciting life. Make a list of all the things you wanted to do while you were married but didn't because you felt your spouse would disapprove. Do them. Was your ex controlling with money? Spend some on yourself. Treat yourself to a new haircut, a facial or massage. Even something simple like a new outfit can make your spirits soar.

You are now in control of your life and get to live it the way you choose. Being single has many benefits. You no longer have to consult with someone else on decisions in your life. You are free to choose for yourself. The best thing about my divorce was the extra closet and drawer space. I liked having that king-size bed all to myself. No more snoring!

Look for the positives in your divorce, and if you think of your marriage, concentrate on the happier moments. Even in the worst of marriages, there had to be some moments of joy. Maybe it was the birth of your children, or when you were newlyweds. If you can appreciate the happier times, you will be able to let go of the bad ones. This is a part of mourning. This is the path to being at peace with your ex-spouse. This is the way to let go of bitterness, hate, and anger.

Although there were painful moments in my marriage, there were some special ones, too, in the early years. Once my husband surprised me with a puppy I had seen in a pet store window. Sometimes he gave me silly little cards expressing his love. He stayed with me during the births of our children and held a bucket to my mouth as I threw up.

Those good times did not last, but if I remember only the bad times, I shortchange the story of my marriage. Over 13 years there were many times of love. We produced beautiful children. The divorce was only a part of it.

You can't reach a new beginning until you leave your old life behind. Your marriage is over. All of the memories are just that: memories. By coming to a place of acceptance you will be able to move on freely and at ease.

When you have truly mourned the end of your marriage, you will know it. You will stop looking at your ex-spouse through a lens of hate and bitterness. He or she will simply be someone you once loved. This is a person that is no longer destined to be a part of your life.

We all begin the divorce process convinced that everything is the other spouse's fault. All of the pain is a direct result of their bad behavior. Your ex is acting in complete disregard for your feelings. If your ex would only behave the divorce would go more smoothly. That you might have a part in this mess doesn't even occur to you. No, your spouse is to blame. He is one who cheated, lied, and betrayed you. How could you be responsible?

But when the dust settles you may start asking yourself some difficult questions. Was it really all your ex's fault? Was there anything you might have done or not done that could have contributed to this divorce?

This is where it gets tough. No one likes to think that they were responsible in any way for the failure of their marriage. It just has to be your ex's fault. Don't you have that long list of sins? How could anyone draw a different conclusion?

Chances are that in most ways you are right, and your ex is wrong. Some of his actions might seem unforgivable. So, after all of the stress, heartache, and pain, why bother to accept any blame?

If you look inward instead of outward, you will be able to take control. With this power you will emerge from your divorce with greater insight and valuable lessons for any future relationship.

Only a victim looks at an ex-spouse and says: "Because of you I do not trust anyone. Because of you my life is empty. Because of you I am in pain." In doing that, the victim gives her ex-husband a controlling power over her behavior. You are making your ex responsible for your life. In saying, "It's not my fault," you are holding yourself back from the hard work of recovery. The longer you harbor this victim mentality, the longer you will deny yourself a chance at the life you deserve to live.

Don't hide from yourself. Dig deep into the memory of your past actions. Look at them, learn from them, and let them go.

Forgive yourself. Until you do that you won't find forgiveness for anyone. Once you do it you might be pleasantly surprised that the anger you feel for your spouse is diminishing.

The willingness to let go of the past, and truly move on to a better place, is the key to peace and happiness.

My self-reflection came slowly and continues to this day. At first I saw my husband's betrayal, lies, and ultimately his anger and violence as the only reasons for our breakup. He had destroyed our marriage. But as I reflected on the whole of our marriage a different picture emerged.

In the last years of our marriage my husband was depressed, lonely, and angry. I saw this and though I took him to a doctor for help, I wasn't as emotionally supportive as I might have been. He was needy. He wanted more than I was willing to give. I thought our marriage was acceptable. I felt no alarm; we weren't in trouble. Yet there he was, telling me he was unhappy. He wanted more from me, mostly affection. I didn't understand.

His depression annoyed me. I felt he should be grateful for the family he had and stop his whining. I was blind. I wanted to believe our marriage was happy.

Through all of this I was denying a memory from years earlier. It was a moment when I had discovered betrayal, and refused to deal with it. I had caught him in a graphic sexual discussion with an employee on the computer. I was seven months pregnant with our fourth child. The evidence stared up at me from the screen. I was stunned. I froze and then started shaking.

When I confronted him he called it a "joke." Did I believe him? Not really, but I pushed the event back in my mind until it lived only in my subconscious. Then I moved on. I should have seen that our marriage had turned into a masquerade.

Through the years my husband's complaints continued. Did I do anything? No. I cut myself off. As I suppressed the memory of his betrayal, I no longer found him attractive. I never connected the two. In bed I would cringe at his touch. I would sometimes stay up, waiting for him to fall asleep so he wouldn't touch me. Yet I felt there was nothing wrong with my marriage.

I was not completely cold to him, we were still affectionate at times, but for him it was not enough. He wanted more.

I occupied myself with reading books, the kids, and our business. I treated him more like a buddy than a husband. I still loved him and cared deeply for him, but I couldn't bring myself to act as a wife should.

When he pleaded and even threatened an end to the marriage, I hardly gave it a thought. I told myself things were fine. He was just a complainer.

When I first suspected his later infidelity my mind flashed back to the earlier incident. In that moment the marriage ended. I snapped. I had always told him that cheating would be the one thing I could not forgive. It was over.

A month before our separation, I found a great deal on a cruise. He wanted it to be just the two of us. Ironically the trip would begin on our anniversary. I insisted that the children be included. He refused to go unless we went alone. He later told me that was the moment he realized the marriage was over. He felt that I did not care about our marriage enough to spend time with him alone.

I know now that subconsciously I too wanted the marriage to be over. However I was not willing to be responsible for it. I would not be the one to blame. That was his role. He was the perpetrator; I was the victim.

To hold on to the illusion of a happy marriage and home life I had to remain blind to my husband's faults, but I also had to be numb to his pain. Without this knowledge about his emotions, I couldn't see him as the man he was.

My husband, feeling unloved and rejected, was easy pickings for a money-hungry tramp looking for an easy ride. She could see what I didn't want to see. She probed the cracks in our marriage and exploited them. By being everything I was not, she brought him down.

This is not to excuse him. My husband was weak. He initiated the affair, and ultimately that is what lost him his marriage. His infidelity was his failure, and his alone. As we've seen, it was not the first time.

You may ask why I would subject the past to so much analysis. Why would I call up the events that caused me such pain?

I do it so that I can be aware, and learn from the past. I do it so that I can see the situation from both sides. I do it to learn. The next time I will have my eyes wide open. I will see people for who they truly are, not who they want me to believe they are.

I am no one's victim. As such, I forgive my ex-husband's infidelities, and I accept responsibility for my own mistakes.

You must reach this point before you can go on. You must remember: accept and forgive. It doesn't mean you want to go back and live it over. It doesn't mean you would keep the marriage together. It means you can move on with your own life, and live with the fact that your ex is doing the same thing.

Your ex-spouse's life is meant to take a different path. If you have children then you will always be part of each other's lives. But you will be able to detach and view your ex as the parent of your children instead of as your spouse. A new relationship will emerge. The roles are different. You choose how you are going to play this out. You can deal with your spouse either with kindness and understanding, having truly put the pain of divorce behind you, or you can harbor ill feelings and hang on to old hurts and feelings of betrayal. The choice is yours. Choose wisely. One road leads to peace and serenity and the other to anger, frustration, and pain.

This is your time of refection and soul-searching. There is light at the end of the tunnel. You will reach it. Right now you may not be able see past the hurt, anger, and pain. But trust me, life will become joyful and complete once again. You get to decide the life you want to have. Don't turn bitter. It may be the easy path now, but later on it will be the hard road, and there won't be any exits. How you see your divorce is the most essential choice you will make.

I now see my divorce for the many gifts it has brought to my life. Amidst the pain and sorrow, I learned some tremendous life lessons. Now I can bring these into my new life and create a more compelling future.

Listen to your heart. Trust in the knowledge that you will survive this devastating loss. You will survive, and you will thrive again.

CHAPTER

10

Helping Your Children Heal after Divorce

There's a fight in the family, maybe as traumatic as a civil war. Mom and Dad have split up. They've fought over income, assets, the house, the bills, and most of all they've fought over you.

That's what a child sees.

They've fought over me.

Like most parents, you will feel guilt. You've heard them talk about it on TV. It's on the radio talk shows. Oprah discusses it, Dr. Phil confronts it, and again and again we hear: the children suffer.

Lately a competing theory has made some waves: Maybe they don't suffer as much as we think. This theory says that if the parents' relationship is unhealthy the kids are better off after a divorce. So which is true? No study applies perfectly to every family, and no theory fits every case, so it depends on you, your ex, and your kids.

My divorce had a huge impact on my four children. My oldest daughter does not speak to her father anymore. In the first year after the separation both my sons had problems in school. My youngest was only six years old. She didn't emerge unscathed. There is no getting around the trauma of the change within my family. My son often tells me that his father and I have ruined his life.

"Are you sad because your Daddy doesn't live with us anymore?" I asked him.

"No," he said. "I'm glad Dad's where he is. He yelled at me a lot when he lived with us. But when we were all there in that house…"

He stopped just as he was getting to the real problem. What my son really doesn't like is that we had to move. In the course of the divorce and its aftermath I sold our house. We couldn't afford such a big place anymore. It's something that happens in many families affected by divorce.

Selling that house broke my heart. I hated taking any of my children away from a place where they had friends and security. I hated disappointing them. Still, as the dust settles, my children are slowly accepting this new home, along with our new family dynamic. We have changed our routines, and with my husband's absence our lives have become more peaceful. After that initial shock, the move, and the gradual readjustment, my kids' grades have begun to come up, and our home has less anger and blame.

Best of all the kids no longer feel as torn as they did when our divorce battle was raging. We've begun to heal.

Although my oldest daughter has chosen not to forgive her father yet, she is doing well in college, and she is in a good relationship. I still have hope that she will find forgiveness for her father for her own sake.

As this healing process begins, you must be realistic about your expectations. It's natural for a parent to be impatient with the slowness of a family's recovery. Remember, you are an adult, and have seen, and perhaps experienced, many of these emotions before. Though you may be going through your first divorce, no doubt you went through breakups in relationships before your marriage. Also, most of us play a role in many divorces, perhaps as a child, and more often as a friend, sibling, or coworker. All of those things plus the simple fact of adulthood prepare us in ways that we can't expect to see at work in our children. Our situation is different from that of our kids in other ways. We rely on marriage for very different things than they do. We saw our marriage as a way to bring them up, and prepare them for the world, and we saw our spouse as a partner with whom to share a life. Parents create a family; children are born into it.

Children see their parent's marriage as something like the roof over their head, the food on the table, and the bed they sleep in at night. Whether they are happy or not, their parents' marriage is "home." It is the thing they return to for nurture, and to them it doesn't make sense that things could go haywire. Isn't growing up crazy enough without this?

You counted on your marriage, but you also saw it ending from the inside out. They are a short step away from that. To put it coarsely, but truly: they are the products of the marriage. So to them your breakup is shattering in a different way. For them it is as if the house caught fire. Now the fire is out, and though the walls are still standing and the rafters are still there, many things must be replaced. Also, some things are gone that are simply irreplaceable. You have seen these fires before, and somehow you know you can go on. They haven't, so they don't.

In some ways your children's emotional roller coaster isn't so different from yours. They need to grieve the loss of the marriage just as you do. They too feel the loss of their family unit. Their loss of a sense of stability is at least as great as yours, perhaps greater.

Once you take these things into consideration you can see how threatening something like the sale of their home would be to them. This is the real house, the real walls, and the real rafters. This is their security. It's hard enough for kids to move when their parents are staying together. When the house goes the way of the marriage, they have to wonder.

It may not be the house. Maybe you can stay where you are. Maybe you have already moved a few times, so leaving doesn't shake them up. But whether they are moving or not, your children's world is changing. It is only natural that they need time to grieve and adjust.

It will show itself in different ways with different kids. Some will act out, express anger, and have trouble in school and/or trouble at home. Your child may say hurtful things to you, blaming you or your ex for the end of the marriage. It is important that you let them get it out. Another child might withdraw or become depressed. All of these emotions are normal. However, if you suspect that your child's reaction to the divorce is extreme, you should consult a health care professional about therapy and counseling.

The nature of your relations with your spouse during the divorce will have a huge impact on how well your children accept it. In *The Truth about Children and Divorce*, Dr. Robert E. Emery tells parents that divorcing mothers and fathers should establish a loving, caring co-parenting relationship early. "Children whose parents put them first from the start have a tremendous advantage," he writes. When you think about it he's only pointing out common sense. You both need to truly put your kids first.

This means working out a relationship with your ex-spouse where the two of you can be parenting partners. This should be done as soon as possible after the breakup. It may require a mediator. It may even need a ruling from a judge. Whatever it takes, do it as quickly as you can, and make sure that you are both on the same page.

Whatever the details of the separation and the divorce, a few major rules should be followed:

1. **Never badmouth your ex in front of your children.**
   Easier said than done. There will be moments when you would like nothing more than to say the worst. Don't! Your children should love both Mom and Dad. It hurts them terribly to hear derogatory comments made about one of their parents. Although it will hurt when a child says: "I want to move to Dad's house," or "Mom's nicer," you have to hold your tongue. Most of us slip up on this one, and certainly that's forgivable. But when you say something bad, do whatever you must to undo the damage.

   You don't have to paint your ex as perfect. Simply explain that while you aren't getting along with their other parent, your child must respect you both. This is when they must take a step in maturity, and learn that not everyone's rules are exactly the same. Remember, a child may forget or forgive a comment made out of anger. But if a parent repeats something, poisoning the child's view of the other parent, it is the child who's damaged.

2. **Do not discuss details of the divorce with your children.**
   They do not need to know about affairs, child support, or any other particulars. Unfortunately my children were exposed to these truths during my divorce. My husband's

mistress moved in with him two months after we separated, so the children knew he was having a relationship with her while he was still married to me. He made comments about certain issues in our divorce. These situations intensified the grieving process for my children in ways that weren't necessary. The effects were devastating. Protecting the children was a challenge, to say the least. If you are in such a situation, you can discuss it with your children, but do your best to step back, be even-handed, and tell only the truth.

3. **Coordinate with your ex, so that you can be consistent about rules and discipline.**

It's inevitable that there will be differences, but narrow them as much as you can. You both may have to give a little. On the most important things (these include matters of honesty, violent behavior, and respect for others) your rules must be the same. Also, it's best if you can coordinate on punishments and restrictions. If the kids are punished and cannot use the computer at Mom's house, then when they go to Dad's that weekend, he must also bar them from using his computer. Such coordination is difficult when there's hostility. Some parents actually enjoy undermining the other parent for revenge. If this happens, try to point out how much this hurts the kids.

Kids need boundaries. Even though they always test the limits, they look to rules for security. If they see that their parents are unified in matters of rules and enforcement, they will feel secure in both households. I counseled a man whose ex-wife openly disagrees and argues about discipline in front of their son. When the son misbehaves, and complains to his mother, she curses at her ex, taking their son's side. This is a no-win situation. The father gets no respect, the mother is using her son to vent her anger (never a smart way to do things), the son loses any bonds he had with his father, and his relationship with his mother becomes one where he is only a tool for her emotional needs.

No matter how ugly the divorce may be, parents need to take a step back. Children must be the top priority. Your child's feelings and needs come before your own. If all else fails, enlist the help of a third party, a teacher or maybe a counselor who can intervene on behalf of your child. Your ex might not realize how his anger affects the children until a professional points it out. The exception to these rules comes if your ex is putting your children in any emotional or physical danger. Then the issue must be addressed immediately and help must be sought.

During my divorce I hired a therapist to help my children deal with the changes in their lives. They expressed a variety of difficulties to the therapist. When it became apparent to me that there were problems with my ex's drinking and certain related behaviors, I found I had an ally in our therapist. When I reported the problems to my lawyer, who went to our judge, the therapist's input gave credence to what I said. A professional outsider can be invaluable in such a circumstance.

Protecting your children is your number-one priority. If you suspect that your ex may be putting them in any sort of danger, you need to report it. Many judges hear tall tales from bitter spouses, so if a professional therapist or counselor can back you up, it helps.

In such a circumstance you must resist any urge for revenge. Though you are dealing with your ex's behavior, remember: your children are involved. They must not become pawns. When you protect your children, remember that they need your spouse too. Do not punish your ex; help him.

Only in cases of sexual or physical abuse, or other clearly dangerous behavior, should you sue for sole custody. This is a last resort. Before you do it, search your soul, and see if you feel your child would be in danger in the presence of your ex. If so, file for sole custody. Custody is for the child; it is not a tool for punishment or revenge. Most things can be worked out amicably. My own ex has corrected some of his behavior, although he still does things that hurt my children's feelings, like not taking them on Father's Day and only seeing them about 48 hours a month. I've heard from the kids that he still smokes cigarettes around them, which drives me crazy, but overall he has been a better father than he was in the past.

Like any children, children of divorce know how to push our buttons. They will wear us down and wear us out if we don't watch ourselves. Also, without even trying, they learn the game of making parents compete. Avoid this. Don't buy them something new just because your ex did. If possible discuss purchases of such things as computers, games, iPods, TVs, vehicles, and just about anything that you may think is questionable from the viewpoint of money or maturity. Don't try to one-up your spouse, and don't try to keep up either. Talk about what your kids should have. Don't let your kids dictate this by playing on your desire to be as good a provider as your ex.

Deep down every child wants parents to be together and happy. The underlying anger at the fact that this cannot happen simmers deep within them and can explode at any time. They might pick fights with their siblings, talk back, get in fights at school, and let their grades drop. They do these things to get attention. The child's world has changed and he doesn't like it. That anger must surface in order for us to deal with it.

Recognize that your child is having problems; do all you can to help. Some children never express their hurt and anger. This follows them into adulthood, showing up in stress-related behaviors and illnesses. Talk to your kids. Let them know it is okay to feel bad, but things will get better. How you behave and carry on with your life will be the direct indicator of how well your kids behave. Show them your strength, and your ability to survive and thrive. Explain that all things, both good and bad, happen for a reason; it's how we deal with them that counts.

It reminds me of the song "Because of You" by Kelly Clarkson. If you have seen the video you know that the song is from the perspective of a child of divorced parents. Their split has left her suspicious and unable to trust. Her mother's bitterness is still a stain on her life.

You are your child's greatest role model. Always lead by example and you will have happy, productive children who will emerge stronger.

The shift from a two-parent home to a one-parent home isn't easy. You will question yourself and the circumstances your children are thrown into. Will they grow up damaged in some way? It's best to remember that no upbringing is perfect. Many children from unbroken homes grow up twisted. I believe that whether you grow up in a home with two parents or one, you will probably be a little screwed up anyway. People aren't perfect, neither parents nor children. We can only try our best.

Ask yourself each day: Am I giving my children a safe, loving home with the things they need to be happy? Do I communicate with them every day, keeping up with their lives and changes? Do I show them love? If you can truthfully answer, "yes" to these questions then you are probably doing a good job as a parent.

The bottom line is that divorce is painful and you cannot completely protect your children from this pain. But you can lessen the risk of emotional damage and raise healthy, happy children even in the face of divorce.

11

Dealing with Friends, Family, and More During Divorce

In a divorce it is not just mom, dad, and the kids who are affected. Your parents, siblings, in-laws, uncles, aunts, and friends are all drawn into the conflict. As you begin the divorce process, your tendency will be to think only of your most immediate world: home, children, and property. This is the core that is changing, but that can blind you to the larger world outside. As the process drags on you will discover that your entire range of relationships has changed. Some of these changes are sudden and huge. Others are far subtler.

Whose friend is whose? Will you ever see your in-laws again? What are the fault lines of your children's loyalties? Will any of their friendships be affected? Much of this turns on the divorce process itself. The nastier it gets, the more difficult these questions become. Can you remain friends with the couple that is still on good terms with your ex? When you're around them do you have to watch every word you say?

As with all issues of divorce, this one is easier if the split is amicable. If you and your ex are on friendly terms, that feeling will usually extend to his relatives.

But if things have been ugly, then relationships change radically. The bitterness in a divorce tends to bleed into far too many other parts of one's life.

If you have things you must fight for—children, a home, a way of life—then a great deal of this is unavoidable. In a fight people take sides. We've all done this with others. I believe my brother, you believe your sister. I trust my old friend, but you trust your old sweetheart, or your golfing buddy, or your coworker. The one you are closer to portrays his wife as the villain, while I believe every word she says about him. Both of us are only getting one side of the story.

When you are one of the people who are divorcing, you suffer not only the loss of a spouse, but a whole set of people you cared about. These may be people you spoke to candidly, folks with whom you shared holidays and vacations. You may have even thought of them as people you would confide in about anything. Suddenly they are cast into an enemy camp, and you wish you'd never said a word to them.

For many of us this is the second stage of heartbreak. We don't realize just how much the underpinnings of our world are built on trust until suddenly a huge chunk of that foundation crumbles. Someone who always smiled when she saw you in the supermarket now turns away. You go to a ballgame, and can't even talk to the couple sitting next to you. It affects everything from what parties you attend, to where you stop the car to wait for your kids after school. It's hard enough seeing the expressions on people's faces. It is even worse when you know they won't even listen to your side. You see them on the street, and know that behind their eyes are a thousand false ideas and impressions. And there is nothing you can do or say to change that.

For years I was close to my mother-in-law. I felt like she was a second mother to me. None of the old mother-in-law jokes or stories applied to us. We talked daily, took trips to Atlantic City together, and went shopping. We could talk about practically anything. When a crisis came I knew that she would be there, backing me up, and I played the same role for her. We both shared a love: my husband. While that might bring out jealousy in some women, it only drew us closer. After a time we shared more interests: the children. We never argued.

At one point I decided I wanted her to live with us. I built an extension on my home and invited her to move in. Looking back, I now see my mistake. Things changed. Soon the old expression about "two women in the same kitchen" rang true.

It took about a year, but then I saw my marriage beginning to come apart. One night at 2 a.m., I got a call that my husband had been beat up after leaving a nightclub. She blamed me, calling me "a cold wife." She later apologized, but it was clear that there was a side of her I'd never known. As the marriage crumbled this side of my mother-in-law came into sharper focus. Our arguments heated to the point where I had to call the police. She said things I could not forget. Now I wanted this woman, who I had cared so deeply for, to leave my home. Our relationship was over.

I had lost my husband and now my mother in-law too. This was my children's grandmother; others soon followed this break. It was what one would expect: his family lining up on his side, my family on mine. His family welcomed his mistress to Christmas dinner: a stranger in my spot.

None of this is easy on anyone. Each moment presents itself, and you feel each slight. For years your life has had a rhythm and ritual that moves through the seasons, with dinners, gifts, weddings, christenings, and all the rites from birth through death, along with holidays and traditions. Then a trusted in-law turns, and within days you realize that a whole world has split off, like a cliff falling into the sea.

The easy thing to say is: be strong. The most important thing to say is: go to the friends and family who have stuck with you. When people turn against you, go to those people who are true to you. Your real friends won't ask you to spell out everything, or to prove anything. They will simply give you love. Always go wherever the love is.

After our divorce was final, things improved a little. I spoke to my mother in-law for the first time, and we managed to be pleasant to each other in front of the children. Among the rest of our families some softened, while others are still angry.

So many aspects of divorce don't end with the two of you. So many others are affected. New partners enter the picture. Inevitably people look at the date you bring to dinner, and compare. This too can be painful. Remember what anyone new in your life has to face in such situations. Though the comparison often works in their favor, being scrutinized is never easy. Also, there will always be those who assume that, if you made a mistake once, this new one must be a mistake as well. Take such attitudes with the grain of salt they deserve.

Sometimes you hear things from your children that they heard from your ex's friends or family. The sting seems amplified. If you hear something that is obviously twisted and wrong, you have a duty to speak up, but even then: keep cool. Sometimes a child is testing the waters, seeing what will make you react. Children do this to see how their changed world is settling. If you are always honest with your children, and make sure they know you are speaking out of love for them, that world will settle into a rhythm where everyone can live a little easier. Remember, your children deserve to maintain a healthy relationship with all their grandparents, aunts, uncles, and cousins.

Even in the worst divorces there has to be a time of healing and acceptance. If you have children, you should do all you can to maintain a civil relationship with your ex and his family. For a time you will feel all the venom that raises in a fight, but once the fight is done, don't hang onto the bitterness. Think of the children. When faced with someone you felt anger toward, force a smile, say hello, and be courteous. You may find that wounds are healing. If not, you won't have deepened those wounds. You do not have to like anyone you don't want to like, just be friendly enough to put everyone at ease.

Forgiveness often grows out of the small things: courtesy, a smile, and a pleasant word. But in the end, no matter how painful, you need to do what is best for the children.

Those of you without children have the luxury of walking away, but in the long run even this can be a trap. While this might seem liberating, hurtful feelings will eventually catch up with you. Unresolved anger will turn into long-term bitterness, spilling over into other areas of life. If you find yourself well beyond a simple, clean, childless divorce, and you still feel hostility and anger, you may need counseling or just a heart-to-heart talk with a friend. Work through the loss you have experienced, grieve for those you have lost, not just your spouse. Try and get to a place of forgiveness or at least indifference. When you no longer feel hate you will be free.

CHAPTER
12

Dating After Divorce

After a divorce finding a new partner is a tricky business. Should you date as soon as the separation papers come through? Should you wait until the divorce is final? How do you know if you're emotionally ready? Choices about dating will vary according to the person and the circumstances of the divorce. There is no absolute formula.

THE FIRST DATE

I didn't date for six months after the separation. During that initial half-year I could hardly think about dating. After the shock of our breakup I passed into an emotional and mental fog. I could make day-to-day decisions, keeping my family together, but I didn't have the strength to even contemplate that first step with a new man.

Time passed, and I began to feel that something was missing. I wondered if a new mate might ease the loneliness. I wanted to test the waters, and I assumed that any man would be seeing it the same way. I had been away from dating for 15 years. I was older, as were most of the men I would date. In those years some basic processes of dating had changed.

Not being sure where to begin, I chose to enlist the help of an online dating service. Soon after joining I was matched with a man, and went out on my first post-marriage date. The man I went out with was nice enough, but he moved too quickly for my tastes. Before we even got to our second date, he had invited me to a family wedding. Our second date turned out to be our last.

The next man I met was also nice. He wasn't as emotionally needy as the first. We had several pleasant times together, but the chemistry wasn't there for me.

The third man turned out to be what we call "the rebound man." This is the man who comes along when the newly divorced woman finds herself wanting to jump into a new relationship long before she's sorted out the emotional debris from the old one. You haven't fully grieved or adjusted; yet without even knowing it, you are desperate to replace what is lost. You invest your hopes in a man before you are ready.

My rebound guy was sweet, kind, and cute. I felt attachment to him from the start. But we had little in common. Our lives had no intersections. Our interests were completely different.

At first I found that easy to overlook. What mattered was he was the opposite of my ex: good-looking, sexy, and a great listener. He listened to all my complaints, letting me vent about my ex, the divorce—everything. Having his attention gave me an emotional lift, making me feel attractive again.

For months I had been beating myself up about my husband's affair with another woman. Was she better looking? More sexy? How could he choose her over me? Now I felt wanted again. He made me laugh.

But our different approaches to life began to show. Our differences became too obvious to overlook. The time came to split, and we both knew it. This breakup wasn't anything like the one with my ex-husband. Besides the fact that there weren't years, children, investments, and the whole of intertwined lives, there was also the fact that we arrived at our decision together. We both understood the problem, and held nothing against one another. We remained friendly throughout.

Still, having yet another breakup so soon after my separation was almost more than I could handle. I panicked. I immediately wanted to find someone else. Fast.

The next man was right around the corner, and another followed right after him. These involved only a few dates. Neither man touched any chord in me. Neither was the kind of man I wanted.

I began to see that in all of this I was only looking for a replacement for my husband. I wasn't leaving room for something different or new. I simply wanted something to fill the empty space—to stop the hurting that was still in me. I had the idea that a man, almost any man, would distract me from the pain. It doesn't work that way. I needed to work through my troubles.

So I took myself off the market. I focused on my divorce. It needed attention, because it was still as ugly and unresolved as it had been a few months earlier. I worked on the legal aspects, preparing for a trial.

Though a trial is usually a confrontation, I also worked along another path. I started reading books on forgiveness. Slowly I tried to rid myself of my anger and hate. Little by little I began to heal. By the time we were set to go to trial, I had begun to feel more at peace. Though sometimes it seemed that my ex would never settle, I kept my wits about me. Finally, only days before the trial was scheduled to start, we came to an agreement.

Now I was free. My life was still a huge mess, but I was liberated from the marriage, so now I had a chance to fix things. I could start with the business, and at the same time fix my family. I also felt as if I could finally pay proper attention to my own emotions. It was time to consider dating again. I was ready, but I was also determined that this time would be different. Now I would take my time, and find the right person.

I approached the whole process with a different attitude, more careful, yet more optimistic in terms of myself. I felt: I am happy with myself, and I don't need a man in any urgent sense. It's true that I would like to find a man with whom I could share my life, but I will start with step one: a single good date that might lead to another. If it didn't, then it was on to the next man. With that I returned to the dating world, looking only for possibilities that were realistic. If someone wasn't right for me, I didn't waste my time with him.

I have met some interesting men, but I am still waiting to really fall in love. This time I know what I'm searching for: the old-fashioned romance of two people madly in love. I am not in a hurry. Instead I am enjoying being single again and meeting new people.

MEETING YOUR NEW MATE

Where do you go to meet someone new? Years ago it seemed like singles bars were the only permanent meeting place. They were open every night, but they were also pressure cookers that were often fueled by too much alcohol. Now there is another spot that is always open: the World Wide Web. The Internet provides many interesting options. As online dating has gained popularity, it has shown itself to be more convenient than singles bars, and offers more possibilities as well.

I joined eHarmony.com. This dating service makes you fill out a lengthy questionnaire aimed at matching you and a mate. The match is made on the basis of several critical components. I liked eHarmony for several reasons. One was their policy of not posting your information and photo for just anyone to see. Your data is sent only to specific matches.

Another popular site is Match.com. Though I made no dates through them, I perused their site, and saw how they worked.

They seem to have a greater selection of potential dates. At Match.com, you can browse and look at available singles' pictures and profiles. You do the choosing using the posted information.

My cousin has had some success there, meeting a man, and starting a serious relationship with him. Hers is one of many Internet success stories. I know of a woman who was recently divorced and developed a friendship online with a man from Scotland. They exchanged emails and photos, and soon their feelings deepened. He sent her two airline tickets to Scotland, one ticket for her and one for a friend. Although hesitant, she went. She fell in love. After returning to the United States she felt that she could no longer go on without this man. She flew back to Scotland and they were married. By the way, he is a millionaire and they live in a castle! They just recently celebrated the birth of their first child. So you see, fairy tales do happen!

For some, nothing will do but to meet someone the old-fashioned way — in person. You can stay away from singles bars but still find people with similar interests by joining a club or taking classes. Even if the right person isn't there, you will still have a lot of fun. The workplace can be an avenue for romance, though you must mind any given job site's rules on socializing.

Although many of us dread singles bars, they can be tolerable, and even good places to go if you take along some friends. Go to one where there's dancing. You may meet someone worthwhile. It does happen!

Last but not least, don't be too shy about having friends or family match you with someone they know.

Whatever option you choose, don't get discouraged. It takes time. If you have the patience you will be rewarded with an array of choices.

YOUR SPOUSE'S NEW RELATIONSHIP

Many of us find a new mate immediately. Your ex-husband may be one of them. This can be hard on you emotionally. My own ex took no break whatsoever. His relationship was the cause of our breakup. She moved in with him two months after he left my home. She left him after a little more than a year. I was elated.

Her departure was satisfying on several levels. My feelings stemmed from my own hurt, and they also came from the disruption and pain she'd brought to my children's lives. But I admit that revenge was a factor. I liked the feeling that my ex was finally getting his comeuppance. Now he would feel the sting of rejection. I wanted him to suffer this. I had good reason. He had thrown out 13 years of marriage, and I wanted him to pay for it.

His girlfriend had been a painful reminder of all that, and I couldn't help but feel relief that her life no longer intersected with mine or my children's.

But these feelings of relief and satisfaction were quickly tempered by the fact that he soon found another girlfriend. I decided that any woman was better than the last, but still I wondered, how could anyone want to date a broke, often unemployed, overweight, balding man?

His new girlfriend was only 24, 14 years younger than he was. She seemed nice enough, but deep down it still bothered me that he was happy. Despite all the books I read about spirituality, forgiveness, and love, I still felt rage.

Try as I might, I couldn't understand these feelings. I no longer had any physical attraction to this man. I didn't even like him. Why would I care? The real reason was that I wanted him to suffer for what he had done to me.

EMOTIONS

It is normal to have confusing feelings long after the divorce is final. An ex's new partner can stir hostility whenever she comes in contact with your children. This is inevitable. Your life has been turned upside down. The familiar and routine are changed forever. Even if your marriage was filled with anger, it was still the life you knew. Some inmates find security in a prison cell. Marriage can be the same.

With divorce new people enter your life, some not by choice. You must find a way to deal with your ex's new love. This is difficult if you are not currently in a relationship yourself. Why him, but not me? you ask over and over.

You feel you are a good person, and you deserve love. You feel as if your ex deserves loneliness and pain. Stop taking it personally. The right person will show up. Though it may not seem so now, he will arrive at exactly the right moment. Be cautious. Look before you leap. There's no need to risk repeating a painful experience. Take your ex's success as an omen. You know that if it can happen to him quickly, you too will find love. If his new love proves fleeting, don't rejoice or worry about it. The longer you wait the better chance you have for a truly lasting love.

Don't jump into something just to prove yourself. This is not a competition. This is a serious search for a love that will last a lifetime. You do not need to suffer again.

That doesn't mean you should ignore your negative emotions. Release them. Talk to a friend or therapist. Punch a pillow. Wait until you are alone, then call your ex every dirty name in the book. Shout it and scream it. Let all of it go. Let go of all of the pain, hurt, and betrayal. The process may take months or even years, but you will feel better in time.

That special someone will come, and your divorce will fade into memory. You will no longer harbor hateful feelings toward your ex. You will come to accept your ex for who he is, and wish him well.

SEX AFTER MARRIAGE

Dating after divorce raises many issues, including sex. What are the rules? If it's been awhile since you were single, a lot has changed.

So what are the new rules? When should you sleep with someone? The third date? Fourth? Longer? Figuring this out is never easy. Will you feel lonely and jump into bed with someone too quickly? Or will you close yourself off emotionally and physically, and make yourself unapproachable? Where is the happy medium when it comes to sex?

When I reentered the dating scene I had no rulebook. Instead I had a friend. She'd been divorced for a year, so I would call her for advice. She said she usually slept with a new boyfriend by the second date. Was this what most people were doing? I had no idea.

I decided she couldn't be my rulebook. I soon discovered there was no rulebook. There are only your own instincts and intuition. When a relationship feels right and you are ready to take the next step, then do it, but do what you can to be sure about your feelings.

Losers are plentiful on the dating scene. Many of these are predators looking for nothing but sex. Don't become the cliché-divorced woman, easy and hungry for sex. Some men look for that. Be careful to avoid these losers.

There are other, even more dangerous newcomers on the dating scene, and they are wound up in sex. It wasn't that long ago that no one had heard of AIDS. There are other, newer sexually transmitted diseases as well, and the predators and losers have new tricks to get what they want.

It is scary out there, for sure. Use common sense. Here are six pointers for getting back in the dating game:

- Always meet in a public place for your first few dates.

- Drive yourself there; do not have your date pick you up at your home.

- Practice safe sex. Always use a condom.

- Do not go back to his home or a motel until you feel you know this man and can trust him.

- Screen him thoroughly. Be choosy. Do not settle for less than you deserve.

- Follow your gut and trust yourself. If something does not seem right about your date, listen to your inner voice.

You can still have a good time and enjoy dating if you follow these simple rules.

YOUR KIDS AND DATING

You may no longer be as single as you once were. Children complicate dating.

While dating a man we'll call "Kevin," I encountered some trying times with my children. Kevin has three small kids, two of them the same age as my three youngest. My boys and his son bonded over video games right away. My youngest daughter loved his daughter and they would play for hours. It all seemed great, but there was one problem. My daughter hated Kevin!

One morning over breakfast she asked him when he was planning on going home.

She would glare at him, and let him know he was not her daddy. Interestingly, my daughter accepted my ex-husband's girlfriend without much problem. I was the one who was not allowed to date! She wanted me all to herself.

One lesson you must learn is: don't introduce your children to your new boyfriend too quickly. When we had a hard time finding babysitters, Kevin and I would frequently bring our children together so we would have time together. When we broke up, both his kids and mine were confused. They still wanted to be friends. I now realize that it was unfair to put my kids in this kind of position. It went both ways. Kevin's kids were still asking to play with my kids months after we ended our relationship.

Another potential problem is the attachment your children might develop to your boyfriend. If things don't work out, then the kids are left with feelings of abandonment by an adult they've grown to trust and love. As you enter into other relationships, their confusion will be compounded.

My policy now is that a new boyfriend doesn't meet my kids until we have been dating for several months. Then I slowly introduce him into their lives. Keeping your boyfriend distant from your children may be tough, but you must think of their feelings.

Kids want mom and dad together. They are often traumatized by the divorce and they will embrace or repel newcomers too quickly. Take it slowly; it will save a lot of heartbreak.

Dating after divorce is an adventure. You will learn new things about yourself and your feelings. Follow your instincts, but remember that a leopard does not change his spots. If a man shows you who he is, believe what's right in front of you. I hope that this advice will steer you away from the losers out there, and that you will meet someone fabulous. It is truly a new chapter in your life. It can bring happiness and joy. Protect yourself and have a good time!

CHAPTER
13

Juggling the Kids, the House, and Your Career Without Losing Your Sanity

When the ink has dried on your divorce papers, and the dust finally starts to settle, you will find yourself facing an entirely new set of problems. Now you are alone with your responsibilities. The scheduling of your life is different and probably more difficult.

If your husband is limited to brief visitation rights, then the day-to-day responsibility for your kids is now completely yours. Even if your spouse has your children part of the time, you will discover that you are more limited. If your ex did anything at all around the house you will now have to do it yourself. If he did any of the family bookkeeping, or helped the kids with schoolwork, or took them here or there, that service is no longer available. You have a household. Once there were two people who could take on the duty of running it. Now there's one.

You will probably begin to see this happening from the start. During your divorce these things present themselves. But in some ways they aren't as obvious then. This is partly due to the incredible turmoil you are already facing. There may also be other factors disguising the truth. Your friends and family knew what you were going through while the battle was still raging. Often some of them stepped up to bat, and helped in so many ways. Your best friend drove your son to sports practice through an entire season, and maybe your sister took your daughter to shop for clothes. But that was when your days were endless cycles of lawyers, court dates, and searching for records. Now life is supposed to be normal.

The only problem with that is the workload: it seems to be permanently bigger.

In most cases the ex-spouse should be of help, but there are almost always problems and disagreements. Most likely these will last as long as your children are still underage and a shared responsibility. How much support and help your ex is giving you with the kids is usually a measure of your sanity. I've had my own problems with this, as does nearly every parent who has custody most of the time. My ex-husband's mandated times with the kids only cover a couple of weekends and some weekday evenings each month. Often the evenings simply don't happen.

Many divorced parents face the same dilemma: doubled responsibility not only for kids, but for shopping, cleaning, paying the bills, taking care of the pets, doing the laundry, and the list goes on and on!

Being a single parent is no easy task. For each of us the new responsibilities take different forms. When they are still together most parents gradually take on some aspects of the good cop/bad cop relationship with their kids. Sometimes dad is the one who is judge and jury, while mom seems willing to listen. Or those roles might be reversed. Maybe your ex-spouse was the disciplinarian; while you were the sympathetic one they could always come to. Whatever role you played before, now you must be both. If your boy gets in a fight, or your daughter mistreats a schoolmate, you have to dole out the punishment. Yet, if there were extenuating circumstances, you also have to understand. How can a person do both? It seems almost impossible.

This is aggravated even more by the divorce. A split inevitably sets up a competitive situation. In a conflict people always look for allies, and in a divorce both parents want the kids to be on their respective sides. This doesn't end with the decree.

If dad was once the disciplinarian, but now only sees the kids for a few days a month, he's likely to be much less help when they do something wrong. He'll want his house to be the place where they have fun. At the same time, mom is going to get tired of always being the one to give punishments. She doesn't want her children to hate her. This often turns into a competition for affection that can only hurt the children.

What every parent in a divorce must learn is that their children still have the same needs they had before the divorce. That means they need the adults in their lives to take on adult responsibilities. For instance, if you are about to drop your children off at your spouse's, don't work extra hard to leave the best impression. There's no need to make your last stop one at a fast food joint where you fill them full of sugar and empty calories. Instead, just make them understand that you love them, and are concerned with their well being in every way. Ease them into the transition by assuring them of their place in your life, while helping them see that they still have that place in your spouse's life as well. If your spouse doesn't cooperate, try to resolve it when the kids aren't there. Do all you can to make sure that the facts of custody are not rules of engagement, but rather are simply a structure for your children's benefit. If you and your spouse still have lingering differences in this area, the best way to help your cause is to simply be the best parent you can be.

But whatever your arrangement is with your ex-spouse, life can't help but be more difficult alone. So what do you do in the face of overwhelming odds, and the seemingly inevitable nervous breakdown?

First, remember you are not alone. There are millions of single parents out there facing the same thing you are. You probably know other mothers (and/or fathers) who are, or have been, in the same situation. Don't be afraid about turning to them now.

They may know things you don't, and if not, they can always lend a hand, or at least some sympathy.

Others who have gone through the same thing will realize what pressure you are under. This isn't simply a matter of finances (though that issue usually has a lot to do with it). You are now the one that your children come to every day of the week. They need you desperately for their own sense of security, especially after their world has been turned upside down from divorce. You are the one who picks up after them, feeds them, and gives them allowances. You are the one who talks to their friends' mothers and fathers. You get the call from school. You talk to their teachers. You are the first one to hear about bills for education and health. If your children are about to go to college, you are the one they talk to about those possibilities.

If you are the parent they stay with most nights, and you are the parent they see in the morning before they go to school, then you are simply the one.

Because it used to be different, because there used to be two of you, and because there used to be two parental roles being played in this house, you now have to learn something new. Now you must develop some skills you never needed before. If you can do what is necessary you'll find that this new order isn't that scary. If you can adapt, you will not only survive, but also thrive. A new exciting life is just around the corner. Your job is to figure out how to keep from getting so exhausted that "just around the corner" turns out to be an impossible distance to cover.

Your job as a newly single parent may not be easy, but it is simple. And it is crucial. You must develop a time management system. Imagine that you have a jar. You also have some rocks, big ones and small ones. You also have sand and water. You need to get all the rocks, sand, and water into the jar. Without really thinking you just start dumping stuff into the jar: some small rocks, some sand, some water—and before you know it nothing else will fit, but you still have most of the biggest rocks on the outside. You look in the jar, and there are big empty spaces. So you dump out what you have, and start over. This time you put in the big rocks first, and then fit in the small ones, pouring the sand and water in between. You put in the last rock, and realize everything fits this time. You can actually try this experiment and see that when you put the big rocks in first everything else will fit.

Think of those big rocks as the important things in your life: time with your kids, a fun night for yourself, time with friends. You might need time for a special hobby, or simply some quiet time to think and focus yourself so that you can pursue your big goals and dreams. Big rocks like these nurture you and make you feel happy and fulfilled. If you put them last in your life, if they just won't fit into your day-to-day activities, then you'll get that nervous breakdown. If you don't put these things first, then a thousand little rocks—the daily events that eat away at your time—will take up every moment. You'll finish each day wondering why the things that are most important to you seem to be slipping away. You'll feel empty, and you'll wonder why. It will be because the small, unimportant tasks have taken up all the room in your life.

The jar is time. The rocks are how you use it. If you develop ways to use time effectively, other things will fall into place.

Developing a schedule and system that works for you can be difficult. The first thing you will need to do is buy yourself a planner. It can be one of those big planner books you buy at an office supply store or you can do it electronically on a palm pilot or even your laptop. Whichever kind it is, it won't do you any good unless you use it. You have to develop "planner habits." That means you have to get in the habit of writing things down. Your planner must have a calendar in it. Use it. Write on it, and refer to it. Look at it every morning. Look at it at lunch. Check it again after work, and before you go to bed at night. Whatever times you choose, make them a part of your habits. Make notes the moment you know that something is coming up. If it's a daily or a weekly event, write it in advance for several weeks at a time. With an electronic planner you can make these kinds of notes permanent. Schedule yourself. As you do this, think of your children, your friends, and your family. Look at your schedule as a way to prioritize. Make sure you are spending the most time with those who are most important to you.

Schedule the most time for the things that are most important—it's a good general rule, but there are exceptions. Though it may sound cliché, there is such a thing as "quality time." Here is an example: say your daughter is going through one of those rough patches most kids have in their teens. This is a moment when she needs her mom. Say you are both morning people. It's over coffee that you think your best thoughts, and can listen patiently. It's with breakfast that she is most able to calmly look at her world. School day mornings are always hurried, so you might want to make sure you have at least one morning you will spend with her every weekend. Or maybe you're both night people. That might make scheduling easier, but you should still be sure you set aside time. Make sure there is a particular evening each week that the two of you will be spending an hour or two alone together. What happens if she's morning and you're evening? There's always a happy medium at some point in the day. Get creative. But remember that this will be important time—not necessarily structured, but set up in a way that encourages real dialogue. It might only be an hour per week, but remember that it is a "big rock."

Think of time in terms of both quantity and quality. Get the most out of each moment. In this way you can juggle time along with the personalities of yourself and your family. Remember you must be your first priority, or you won't have any priorities at all. Your time is precious, so you need to schedule it wisely.

Try the "big rocks" principle with your calendar. Fill in your "big rocks" first. I learned this system from a seminar I attended called "Life Directions" by the Peak Potentials Training Company. If you would like learn more about this company email them at info@peakpotentials.com (use reference number 142363). I found it worked for me, and you may find that it works for you. Whatever system you use, prioritizing is the most essential skill you will need in organizing your life, and a calendar is the key to prioritizing. If you can do this you will accomplish more, and enjoy your life more. You will be able to thrive as a single parent.

Using the big rocks principle, your schedule may look something like this:

MONDAY........... *Call a friend*

TUESDAY .... *Read a book*

WEDNESDAY ...... *Craft night*

THURSDAY .... *Dinner out*

FRIDAY........... *Date night*

SATURDAY .... *Fun with kids*

SUNDAY .... *Open*

Once you've prioritized and scheduled relaxing activities, fill in your planner with all those small rocks: work, chores, errands, cleaning, laundry, etc. We've already mentioned morning and night people. Do you have a more productive time period in the day? I am at my most creative and energetic from 11 at night until 1 in the morning, but it's best if I have those hours to myself most nights. That's when I write and work on business projects. When is your peak time? Often this is the best time for those activities that bring you personal focus.

Whatever method you use, prioritizing is essential to being a single parent. Some people are naturals at this. A lot of us aren't. If you fall into the latter category, look for tried-and-true ways that have worked for others. I'll start you off with one:

Karen Argabright, a member of the Freehold Toastmasters International in New Jersey, recommends the ABC method to prioritize your tasks:

A. *MUST get done*
B. *SHOULD get done*
C. *IF it gets done this week that's okay.*

This method eliminates much of the guilt we often feel when we do not accomplish everything on our to-do list. If you review your schedule and find that there are things you just don't have time for this week, then postpone things in category C. Just remember your big rocks; those are the As on your list!

HERE ARE A FEW OTHER TIPS:

- Time your phone calls. How many times have you spent hours chatting on the phone, only to hang up and realize that you don't have time to do what you wanted to do? Set a timer by the phone. When it rings, politely tell the caller that you must hang up. You feel more in control and have more time to accomplish your goals.

- Clean out your kids' book bags once a week. Take school notices and put them in a folder. At that moment go through the folder and throw out anything that does not need to be answered. Take action on all the other letters and write those checks to the PTA and book club now before you forget!

- Set your kids' clothes out every night for school the next day. If you have very young children, you can save time by dressing them in their school clothes after the evening bath and letting them sleep in them. The clothes will be clean, although maybe a little wrinkled, and you can head out the door that much faster.

- Review your schedule every morning and evening. Make modifications for things that may come up unexpectedly.

- Schedule a specific time to answer your email.

- Clean your house and do laundry every day, instead of once a week. It is much easier to throw a load of laundry in while watching TV in the evening than to be overwhelmed with tons of it on the weekend. Assign a cleaning task each day, such as: Monday, bathrooms, Tuesday, vacuum, Thursday, kitchen, etc. By breaking down the big tasks you will be less overwhelmed and your house will be a lot cleaner!

- Give those kids some chores! Even a young child can help fold laundry and clear the dinner dishes from the table. Have your family help out; after all they live there too!

- Be ruthless with your time! Try scheduling one hour a day for focus time: your time to decide on what is important to you.

- And remember to reward yourself. It can be anything, big or small, that refreshes you and that you enjoy.

Another important idea is to surround yourself with things you love. Make your home your haven: a place to relax and escape from the daily stresses of your life. You might say: "How can I relax in my house when it is a mess?" You have a point. If your home is filled with clutter and disorder, then it will be hard to enjoy it.

Clutter saps your energy, and is a wall against the good things in life. Whatever system you use, remember, your home is the most important place in your life, and in the lives of your children. It should be a place that all of you can feel good about.

When considering the state of your house, the first thing to do is evaluate the situation. Assess what parts of your house need the most work. Get out a pad and pen and write down the following:

For $297 in free bonuses go to www.secretsofdivorce.com/2bonuses.htm

ENTRANCE OF HOUSE	CABINETS
LIVING ROOM	DESK
BEDROOMS	PAPER
LAUNDRY	CAR
BATHROOMS	GARAGE
KITCHEN	STORAGE SPACE

Now rate each area for organization and neatness on a scale of 1 through 10, 10 being the highest and 1 the lowest. Number 1 is what needs the most improvement. Start there. Focus on that place only. You will need garbage bags and boxes for storage. Go through each item in that area and ask yourself: Do I really want to keep it? Will I use it? Does it serve my higher good to keep it? If you can't answer those questions, throw it out.

Things that you use often need specific places. Put things in the proper locations. Put the rest in the storage boxes and label them. Get rid of anything that is broken, chipped, dirty, or just not useful. You want to start bringing good, positive energy into your home; hanging on to clutter only drains you.

There is also the clutter that seems to cling to tasks. This is more emotional than physical. What tasks do you like the least? These are challenges. Make a list of your biggest challenges. Is it managing your bills and other paperwork? Keeping the house clean? Laundry? For me, food shopping, cooking, and cleaning are my biggest challenges. I just hate to cook! Ditto for food shopping. I do not really mind cleaning, but I hate it when the kids mess up the house right after I finish. I figured there had to be a better way.

One thing I discovered was online food shopping. Check your area to see if this service is available to you. I use www.peapod.com. You can shop for virtually all of your groceries from your computer. The groceries are priced slightly higher and there is a delivery charge, but if you're ordering for a family it's not much more, and everything is delivered to your door (or even into your kitchen). The only drawback I have found is that sometimes they run out of an item, and you don't find out until your order arrives.

Providing for and running a household alone can be daunting. Approach it with a sense of humor, and go with the flow. Even with the best-laid plans, things will always go wrong. That is just how life is. The difference is in how you react to it. If you're enjoying life in general, the snags are much easier to take. So are the mundane chores. When you have order and calmness in your life, you are better equipped to handle the little daily disasters. If you can rid your life of general chaos, your days will soon be filled with the "Big Rocks" that give you pleasure, and all those other things will miraculously fit in!

CHAPTER

14

How to Rebuild Your Life Financially in Three Easy Steps

Your financial situation after a divorce depends on these factors: support and settlement payments, job status, business opportunities, time, assets, and the financial needs of you and your family. Traditionally, stay-at-home moms have had the most difficult transition after a divorce. Usually the stay-at-home mom suddenly has to find work. Most likely you did have a job before you had kids, and your first thought might be to go back to your old workplace and see what's available.

Then you often come up against the ladder model. This is the way many businesses operate. You climb up one rung at a time, but if you get off the ladder you land at the bottom again. When a woman quits her job, and goes home to raise the kids, she loses her place in the business world. She not only misses out on promotions; she often won't even be able to walk back into the job she left. She's gotten off the ladder. This doesn't mean things are hopeless, but many stay-at-home moms have a lot of catching up to do, and there is no way to entirely escape the effects of lost time.

If your divorce settlement left you rich, then you might not have to worry about this. The rest of us do. Even with a job or small business, and even if you get some support payments from your ex, being a single parent costs more. Your finances will be disrupted, and adjustments will have to be made.

Your job, your ex's job, and the details of the settlement all work together to paint your financial picture. If they add up to enough money for everything, you can skip this chapter. If not, then read on.

The days and weeks after a breakup can be frightening, and every bill can create panic. Things can get even scarier after the final decree if your settlement is small. At such moments you should take a deep breath, calm yourself, and take a hard look at your resources. You must consider:

1. Earning a living: your options for earning a living day-to-day, week-to-week, year-to-year.

2. The credit crunch: How can you repair bad credit? How can you get out of debt? How can you create new credit in your own name?

3. How you think about money: Spending and saving. Often this has to change.

EARNING A LIVING: STARTING A NEW
CAREER OR A NEW BUSINESS

For most of my marriage I was a stay-at-home mom to our four children. I'd given birth to my eldest daughter when I was 18, and from then on I was headed toward life as a housewife. I never went to college. In those early years I did have a few jobs in sales, but they weren't permanent, and as we had more children, I became more attached to our home. My husband got a well-paid job as a network analyst, and there didn't seem to be much need to work. I knew there might be good reasons to keep a foot in the work world, but kids keep you busy, and somehow I never thought any of those reasons would apply to me.

Finally, when my youngest child was a year old, I started to head back into the workplace. My husband and I owned a salon, and I began to work there part-time. The job went well, and I took on more hours. Soon we bought another salon, and merged it with the first one, enlarging the business considerably. I ran the business while my husband continued his work in the computer field.

The money I brought home was hardly enough to support four kids and myself. It was my husband's income that made the difference. So when we broke up I began searching for ways to make more and spend less. As the divorce proceeded I realized my ex was going to fight me for it. The salon was all I had, yet he wanted it. I had no marketable skills, little education, and the one business I knew was that salon. Without my husband's income life was becoming incredibly scary. Without the business life would become impossible.

The business made a small, regular profit, but even that couldn't begin to support all five of us. Still, I knew if I had the business it could help us get by until I could sell it. In the end I managed to get the salon and a year after my divorce became final I sold it. But it was a long slide across very thin ice.

I was in the same position as so many of you: short on skills, experience, and education, and looking for whatever work a high-school grad can get. In such a world you wind up grateful for $10 per hour. Then you wonder where you'll get the $8 per hour for daycare.

So why bother working at all?

Work because there are ways to make more than $10 per hour. You simply have to find them. Here are three steps you can take:

1. Assess your skills. What have you learned in your years in the home? Is there any part of being a housewife and mother that you're particularly good at? Something people pay for? Something you like? Or was there any particular thing you were good at back when you worked? Something you could develop now, and quickly develop into a service with a market? It's important that it be something you like. I don't believe you can be happy working full-time at a job you hate.

Make a list of all of the things you enjoy doing. Might there be a job in a field that could harness your natural talents and pay you a decent salary? For example, let's say that you love to plan parties. Could you get a job in a party planning company? A catering hall? How about working in a hotel as an event planner? Do you love kids? How about running a daycare center out of your home? That way you do not have to pay a sitter. (But be careful of the daycare option; it's an idea that occurs to so many single mothers, and the field is often crowded. Before you get a license, make sure you have customers.)

I could give you example after example here but the point is to find something you enjoy and find a way to incorporate that into your work. If you are marketing your skills, remember to be businesslike about it. This applies to appearance, courtesy, and confidence, but it also means watching the bottom line. Always look at what you are spending, what you are getting for it, and how much profit you're making.

2. Assess your education. Do you already have a college degree or some other training? Can you go back to school to learn a trade? There are many short-term courses out there that can have you earning money in no time. A typical realtor's course is only a few weeks of full-time attendance. A hair stylist can get a license in most states

in nine months of full-time schooling, and it's a job where you can make terrific money. At my salon the stylists made much more money than I did! Most hairdressers get high commissions and make a lot in tips. For the most part they set their own hours.

Check into other programs that can get you certified in a short time. Schools offer refresher courses in many skills. When my ex complained that he had been out of the computer field for too long and couldn't find work, I called the school where he had learned his skills years earlier—the Chubb Institute. They offered free refresher courses and job placement. See if you qualify for such a program. We never know until we ask. But most importantly, pick something you have an interest in and that you will do well.

3. Think about starting your own business. Many businesses can be started on little or no money. In the past I have sold children's clothing on eBay, and the eBay business model works for a lot of services. In many cities, people offer to clean out garages and attics, selling the contents on eBay, and splitting the profits 50/50 with the owner. I found a huge demand for used children's clothing. Most of us throw our kids' clothing into donation bins. You can sell those clothes on eBay and make money. All you need is a computer and a digital camera. Ask friends

who are discarding their hand-me-downs to give them to you instead.

This also applies to antiques, collectibles, and other valuables. People have so many things they would love to get rid of but they don't have the time. There are other options. Many women have begun cleaning homes or businesses, and soon find themselves employing others to do the actual cleaning, while they price jobs, do the hiring, and inspect the work. Of course there are countless small business ideas that you can do right from your home. Be creative. If it seems sensible, team up with a friend or partner. Owning your own business can be fun, profitable, and boost your self-esteem. It can also get you tax breaks, freedom from bosses, and it may even make you rich.

THE CREDIT CRUNCH: HOW TO GET OUT OF CREDIT CARD DEBT AND REPAIR YOUR CREDIT SCORE

Rebuilding your life financially is never easy. Count on spending a lot of time and effort on this, especially if you went into debt during the divorce process. As I have noted, there were times when I paid my attorneys with credit cards. When the dust of my divorce battles finally cleared I was mired in debt. It took me awhile to straighten out my finances, but ultimately I was able to regain my financial health.

Have you rung up huge debts on the plastic? No matter how bad it looks, there are ways out. You just have to find the one that's most sensible and realistic for you. If you received an asset like the marital home, you could refinance it and then negotiate payoff settlements with your creditors. Usually credit card companies will only talk to you about this option after you have stopped paying your bill each month and it has gone into collection. If it's clear that you can't pay it all, most of them will settle for anywhere from 50% to 70% of the debt. But remember if you haven't been able to make payments, a large amount of what is owed is interest and late fees. You can also call your credit companies and ask them if they have any "plans" for hardship cases. If you tell them your story, they will most likely offer you a plan with reduced monthly payments and a lowered interest rate. If you are in a position to pay your credit card bills, and your credit is still good, make sure you ask for a reduced interest rate. Take advantage of balance transfer offers for lower rates. But be careful to note when these rates will expire. Usually the interest will balloon back up. You will then need to transfer the balance again to a lower rate.

Your credit rating is the key to your financial health. Poor credit scores can raise your car and home insurance rates. I got socked with a $4,000 car insurance bill because my credit score had tanked, yet I had never been late on an insurance payment. When I wrote them explaining how my difficult divorce had lowered my credit rating, they reduced my premium. Without good credit you will pay much higher interest on refinancing your home, car loans, or any other loan. In some cases you may need a co-signer.

Divorce sent my credit score into the toilet, and at the time there was little I could do. Even when I started making regular payments and settling debts, the mark remained on my credit. Repairing broken credit takes time, but if you stick with a plan and pay everything on time, it will happen.

But what do you do in the meantime? Everyone needs a credit card for emergencies. If you do not have one the next option is a debit card. Also you might ask a close relative if they would mind making you an additional cardholder on one of their accounts. Assure them this card will be for emergencies only. Always pay for whatever you charge immediately. You can only ask this of someone you are very close to. It's one of the biggest financial favors one can do for another: putting their credit on the line for you.

If you can do it, take out a secured loan from a bank. Here is an example of how it works; you put $1,000 in a one-year certificate of deposit with your bank. The bank then gives you a $1,000 loan for one year at 9% interest. If you make the payments each month, at the end of the year you can cash your CD in and earn some interest. Current interest rates for a CD are now about 5%. This improves your credit rating because the bank will report to the credit bureaus that you paid off the loan.

When you are starting to rebuild from a credit disaster you should get a current copy of your credit report and check it for errors. Make sure any debts that were ruled to be your ex-husband's in your final divorce decree are off of your credit report. You are entitled to one free credit report per year, and you can also get a free report if you have been denied a loan, line of credit, or other financial service. You can pay for a copy of the report at any time.

GAINING CONTROL: HOW TO CONTROL YOUR MONEY, HOW TO CONTROL YOUR THOUGHTS

There are countless books on how to get rich. We buy them for hope, but the best of them offer us a mindset. If you want to make money you have to think like someone who makes money.

One book that has really helped me change the way I think about money is *Secrets of the Millionaire Mind* by T. Harv Eker. This book encourages you to explore what you learned from your parents about money. You learn what your "financial blueprint" is for success. This book taught me a system for saving money.

Eker's system involves setting up a number of jars, and putting money into them each week. One jar is labeled "Financial Freedom." That money is only for investments that will bring you passive income. There are other jars for "Long-Term Savings," "Education," and "Give Away." The last jar is everyone's favorite: the "Play" jar. That's money you're required to spend on yourself. You're supposed to use it to treat yourself to something luxurious— a massage or an expensive dinner—something a rich person would buy. The idea is to set aside 10% of each paycheck in each jar. If that's too much, you at least put in something—whatever you can afford on a regular basis. The important thing is the habit. I used this system, and it gave me the security of knowing that at least I had control of some of my money. If you would like to learn more about this system and get a copy of this life-changing book go to: www.secretsofthemillionairemind.com/a/successfuldivorce.

I am a firm believer in the Law of Attraction: whatever you pay attention to will expand. If you constantly complain about debts, they will grow. It's like the bad day that always gets worse: you stub your toe, the dog throws up, the kids start fighting, and by the end of the day you're lucky if a tractor-trailer hasn't smashed into your house. Bad luck seems to create more bad luck. The key is to stop as soon as it starts happening, and change how you think and feel. So you stub your toe. It hurts, but you get over it. The dog throws up? Clean it up and move on. The kids fight, so you break it up and send them to school. Find and hold on to a positive attitude.

But, you say, you don't live in my house! Easier said than done!

True, but let me give you a trick that will usually get you out of a bad mood: Be grateful. Think of everything that you have and who you love. Feel the feelings of joy and love you get from having those people in your life. Be grateful for your pets, your house, your car, a sunny day, a rainy day, anything and everything! It is amazing how good you will feel by doing this every day. More of those good feelings and thoughts will flow your way.

The same idea applies to money; the law of attraction can bring you great abundance. Each day visualize what you want. "See" that house you want, or the car, or whatever. Be in the moment and actually see yourself enjoying these things. Feel how good it feels. Make a "Dream" Board. Cut out pictures of the things you want and stick them on a corkboard or poster. Look at this daily. Before you know it you will begin to attract these things into your life. Believe me, it works!

Two terrific books about the law of attraction are Joe Vitale's *The Attractor Factor* and Esther and Jerry Hicks's *Ask and It Is Given*. An amazing movie you can order online called *The Secret* (http://www.thesecret.tv/home.html) also explains how the law of attraction works. Take this seriously; it will change your life. By bringing more to your life, you will enjoy life more and be less stressed.

These fundamentals will improve your life financially. Study wealth. There is so much great information out there. Read everything you can. Continue to learn. I am addicted to learning and I love to read. If you aren't fond of reading, then listen to audios in your car, and watch informational DVDs. Open yourself to new ideas. You will see dramatic changes in your finances. Apply the principles you like, and disregard the rest. Continue this quest and in time you will have everything that you desire!

Conclusion

Congratulations! You have now learned the secrets to a successful divorce. I hope that this book has armed you with the tools you will need to get the best divorce settlement possible. In this book I guided you through the decision-making process and gave you critical information for protecting yourself legally and financially. I also gave you detailed strategies on how to win in the courtroom and find a great attorney.

I hope that you study what is in this book and follow it. Realize that everything is at stake now. Your future depends on the actions you take now. Divorce is never a pleasant experience but I hope that the information presented in this book will comfort you and give you hope. Even the nastiest divorces can be successful in the end. I am a living example!

One day soon this divorce will be over and a new chapter of your life will begin. It may seem so far away for those of you just beginning your divorce or who are in the process of divorce. Some of you reading this are already divorced and dealing with the aftermath and the many questions that arise. So when your divorce truly "ends" will depend entirely on you. Your divorce is not over on the day that the judge signs your final divorce order. It ends when you have straightened out your financial affairs. It ends when you no longer look at your ex and are filled with rage and hate. It also will be over when you have learned to rely on yourself and find out that you actually enjoy your own company.

You are an independent, strong woman who has been through an emotionally draining, life-changing ordeal. But guess what? Your divorce has now made you a stronger person. Someone who can handle anything life throws her way.

You may be reading this and thinking that you do not feel very strong right now. Your divorce may have appeared to take the life out of you. But do not be fooled. Just when you think you cannot take anymore, you find your inner strength and you are amazed at what you can do.

I remember feeling that my divorce would never be over, that I would be stuck in a financial and emotional limbo forever. It took eighteen long months from the date I filed until I was legally divorced. Eighteen months of hell. Toward the end, I felt like I was losing it. I did not think I would survive financially but I somehow pulled myself together and found the resources to hang on. Being able to hang on and not crumble is ultimately what "won" me my divorce. My ex ran out of money, his girlfriend left him, and he gave up his fight and settled. I will never forget that day in the conference room of my attorney's office. We were finally negotiating a settlement. My ex turned to my lawyer and me and said, "Why don't we just split everything down the middle?" I nearly fell off my chair. That is all I wanted to do from day one! He refused. He felt I wasn't entitled to a

50/50 split. I owed $40,000 in attorney's fees and was deeply in debt. If we had settled in the beginning, our attorneys' fees combined would have helped put one of our kids through college! What a needless waste of money. But you can't change the past and live by "what could have been or should have been." You have to move on and cut your losses.

If you were to ask my ex who came out the winner in our divorce, I am sure he would go on at some length about how I got "everything." But in reality how can there be a winner when there was so much pain and heartache involved? We often measure "winning" in financial terms. But what are the emotional costs? Remember to look at both the financial and emotional price tags when considering your settlement. Ask yourself if it is emotionally worth it to fight it out for a few more dollars. It may be. It all depends on your individual situation.

Your emotional and physical well being are of the utmost importance. Never sacrifice your health or your sanity. In the chapter on "Mourning the Death of Your Marriage," you were given advice on how to finally let go and move on. This will take time. Give yourself permission to go slowly and move through the process. Soon enough you will begin to let go.

Eventually you will want to consider dating again and you learned the key elements of reentering the dating scene. Wait for that someone special; never settle! Consider this piece of advice: no matter how attracted you are to someone, if you do not have a common interest and are not on the same path in life, it probably will not work. Look for a soul mate who enjoys the same interests you do. Most importantly do not rush into a new relationship. Divorce wounds take time to heal.

I wrote the chapters "Juggling the Kids, the House and Your Career without Losing your Sanity" and "Three Easy Steps to Rebuilding Your Life Financially" because I want you to know that it is possible to be a great single mom and support your kids. It is not always easy and there are plenty of times when your patience is tested. But you will find yourself starting to enjoy your new life with your kids. Life as a single mom is often chaotic and filled with many adventures. In time you will adjust to running your household alone without your ex and you may even enjoy it.

I want to thank you for reading this book. I wrote this book because I did not want another woman to go through what I did during my divorce. This is the book I wish I could have read and learned from. It would have saved me a lot of money and heartache.

I am a single, divorced mom just like you. I am learning every day and doing the best I can to raise my four children as a single parent. I would like to invite you to visit my website at www.secretsofdivorce.com so that we can continue our relationship. I would love to meet you someday at a seminar, through my coaching program, or anywhere that destiny might bring us together. Please let me know if there is anything I can do to help you. Being divorced women, I believe we share a common bond

and need to network together and share our ideas. I will be add-
ing a forum to my Website where divorced women can discuss
and share their feelings, insights, and receive advice.

I wish you the best of luck,

Christina Rowe

Claim Your Two
FREE BONUSES Now!

$297 VALUE

If you are thinking about getting divorced, are in the process of a divorce right now or if you are already divorced the following two valuable bonuses are guaranteed to help you.

BONUS #1

The first bonus is a 20 minute phone consultation with Christina Rowe. Christina will answer your questions personally and give you the advice you need. This is a rare opportunity to speak one on one with the author.

BONUS #2

The second bonus is a subscription to Christina Rowe's Secrets of Divorce Newsletter. This online newsletter will keep you updated and informed on the latest divorce strategies. Christina will be consulting with top notch experts in legal, parenting, financial and other related fields. She will bring you the very best tips and techniques you need for a successful divorce!

TO CLAIM BOTH BONUSES GO TO:

www.secretsofdivorce.com/2bonuses.htm

OR MAIL OR FAX THE FOLLOWING INFORMATION:

Name

Email address

Phone number

Fax: 732-879-0233

Mail to:

Christina Rowe

3171 Route 9 North, #321

Old Bridge, NJ 08857-2690